POWERSHELL CAN'T GET EASIER THAN THIS

Automate Tasks, Boost Efficiency, and Simplify Server Management

A Comprehensive Guide to Streamlining IT Workflows, Diagnosing System Issues, and Enhancing Efficiency

Richard B. Statler

Copyright © 2024 by Richard B. Statler.

All rights reserved. No part of this publication may be reproduced, distributed, or transmitted in any form or by any means, including photocopying, recording, or other electronic or mechanical methods, without the prior written permission of the author, except in the case of brief quotations embodied in critical reviews and certain other non-commercial uses permitted by copyright law.

Disclaimer:

The advice and strategies contained herein may only be suitable for some situations. This work is sold with the understanding that the author and publisher are not engaged in rendering professional services. If professional assistance is required, the services of a competent professional should be sought. The author and publisher specifically disclaim any liability incurred from the use or application of the contents of this book.

Acknowledgments

I would like to extend my heartfelt thanks to everyone who contributed to making this book possible.

First and foremost, I would like to thank the Lord Almighty for His reassuring grace and my family for their unwavering support, patience, and understanding as I spent countless hours researching, writing, and refining this material. Your encouragement and belief in me have been a constant source of motivation.

A special thank you to my colleagues and mentors in the IT field who have shared their invaluable knowledge and experiences with me over the years. Your insights have shaped my understanding of the IT industry, and your willingness to collaborate has been instrumental in the development of this book. To those who reviewed early drafts and provided feedback—thank you for your keen eyes and thoughtful suggestions. Your contributions have helped me ensure that this book is both technically accurate and accessible to a wide audience.

I would also like to express my gratitude to the wider PowerShell community. It is through your discussions, questions, and shared solutions that I have continually learned and refined my own expertise. Your passion for automation, problem-solving, and sharing knowledge inspired me to create this book.

A special mention goes to [insert names of specific individuals—e.g., fellow authors, editors, or technical reviewers] who contributed their time and expertise to help make this book a reality. Your efforts have truly made a difference.

Finally, I would like to thank you, the reader, for choosing this book as a resource on your journey to mastering PowerShell. I hope you find the knowledge and tools within these pages both useful and inspiring as you work to optimize your IT operations.

Thank you all for your support and for being part of this endeavor.

— **Richard B. Statler**

Table of Contents

Acknowledgments 2
Introduction 12
Chapter 1 20
Understanding PowerShell Fundamentals 20
   What is PowerShell? 21
      A Brief History of PowerShell 22
      PowerShell vs. Traditional Command-Line Tools (CMD, Bash) 22
   PowerShell Syntax Basics 24
      Cmdlets 25
      Pipelines 25
      Objects 26
      Aliases 27
      Parameters 28
      Variables 29
   PowerShell Environment 30
      PowerShell Console vs. Integrated Scripting Environment (ISE) 30
      Setting Up and Customizing PowerShell 31
   Introduction to PowerShell Scripting 36
      Writing Basic Scripts and Running Them 37
      Error Handling and Debugging Basics 39
Chapter 2 46
PowerShell Core Concepts and Language Features 46
   Variables and Data Types 46
      How to Declare and Use Variables 47

    Key Data Types... 48
    Type Conversion..52
Control Flow and Logic..53
    Conditional Statements (if, else, switch)....................53
    Loops (for, foreach, while)... 56
    Error Handling (try/catch/finally)................................ 58
Working with Objects..62
    Understanding Objects, Properties, and Methods..... 62
    Using `Get-Help`, `Get-Command`, and `Get-Member` to Explore Objects... 65
    Practical Example: Exploring a File Object................68
Creating and Using Functions.. 69
    Syntax and Best Practices for Defining Reusable Functions... 70
    Function Parameters and Return Values...................73
    Function Scope and Variables................................... 78
    Best Practices for Working with Functions................ 79

Chapter 3...82
Automating IT Tasks with PowerShell................................82
    Managing Files and Directories with PowerShell............ 83
        File Operations.. 83
        Directory Management... 86
        Advanced File Operations... 90
    Working with the Windows Registry Using PowerShell... 92
        Reading from the Windows Registry......................... 92
        Writing to the Windows Registry................................95
        Common Registry Tasks with PowerShell................. 99
    Process and Service Management with PowerShell..... 102
        Viewing and Managing Running Processes............ 103
        Managing Windows Services...................................107

Common Service and Process Management Scenarios.. 112
Working with Event Logs in PowerShell........................ 113
Viewing Event Logs... 114
Creating Custom Event Logs................................... 118
Automating Event Log Monitoring............................122
Task Scheduling and Automation with PowerShell........ 125
Scheduling Tasks with Task Scheduler Using PowerShell..126
Automating Regular IT Maintenance Tasks............. 130

Chapter 4... 136
Troubleshooting Servers Using PowerShell.................. 136
Network Troubleshooting.. 137
Testing Network Connectivity with `Test-Connection` and `Test-NetConnection`... 137
Working with Network Adapters and IP Configurations. 139
Disk and Storage Troubleshooting............................... 142
Querying Disk Information (`Get-Volume`, `Get-Disk`).. 143
Identifying Disk Space Issues and Generating Reports 147
Additional Tips for Disk and Storage Troubleshooting... 149
Service and Application Monitoring............................... 151
Checking the Status of Critical Services................... 152
Monitoring Application Logs and Performance Counters.. 155
Server Health and Performance.................................... 161
Using `Get-Process` for System Diagnostics........... 161
Using `Get-EventLog` for System Diagnostics........ 164

Using Performance Counters for Server Diagnostics.... 166

Generating Server Health Reports.......................... 169

Automating Troubleshooting Tasks................................171

Creating Scripts to Automate Common Troubleshooting Actions... 172

Setting Up Alerts for System Failures or Performance Issues... 175

Scheduling and Automating Troubleshooting Tasks 178

Chapter 5...182
Managing Users and Active Directory with PowerShell 182

Creating and Managing User Accounts........................ 183

Creating New User Accounts...................................183

Modifying User Accounts... 184

Deleting User Accounts... 185

Bulk User Creation from CSV Files....................... 186

Managing Active Directory Groups................................ 188

Adding Users to Active Directory Groups................ 189

Removing Users from Active Directory Groups....... 191

Managing Group Membership and Permissions......192

Automating Active Directory Tasks................................ 197

Automating Password Resets.................................198

Automating Group Membership Changes............... 199

Scripting User Reports..201

Active Directory Health Checks.............................. 203

Querying AD Data... 205

Retrieving User Data with `Get-ADUser`................. 205

Retrieving Group Data with `Get-ADGroup`............ 207

Retrieving Organizational Unit (OU) Data with `Get-ADOrganizationalUnit`.....................................208

Filtering AD Data... 209
Exporting Results to CSV or HTML Reports............211
Advanced Filtering and Queries............................... 212

Chapter 6..216
Reporting and Auditing with PowerShell......................... 216
Generating System Reports:... 216
Creating Custom Reports for Servers, Users, and Network Devices..217
Exporting Reports to CSV, HTML, or PDF Format.. 219
Audit Logs and Security Monitoring...............................222
Using PowerShell to Query Security Logs and Perform Audits..222
Tracking User Activity, Login Attempts, and Failed Processes...225
Performance and Health Reports.................................. 228
Automating the Generation of System Health and Performance Reports...228
Creating Alerts for Critical Thresholds and Automated Responses...231
Scheduled Reports... 235
Setting Up Scheduled Tasks to Automatically Generate and Send Reports...................................235

Chapter 7..242
PowerShell Best Practices for IT Operations.................. 242
Writing Clean and Maintainable Scripts........................243
Code Structure, Comments, and Naming Conventions. 243
Script Modularity and Reusability............................ 245
Using Version Control for Scripts...................................250
Best Practices for Managing PowerShell Scripts with Git or Other Version Control Systems.......................251

8

Error Handling and Debugging...257
   Advanced Error Handling Strategies and Logging.. 258
   Debugging Techniques for Complex PowerShell Scripts..262
Optimizing PowerShell Scripts for Performance............267
   Performance Considerations and Best Practices for Efficient Script Execution..268
   Minimizing Memory Usage and Optimizing Loops and Queries...272

Chapter 8...280
Advanced PowerShell Techniques and Automation......280

PowerShell Remoting..281
   Enabling PowerShell Remoting................................281
   Executing Remote Commands with `Invoke-Command`..282
   Interactive Remote Sessions with `Enter-PSSession`... 284
   Running Scripts Remotely...285
   Credential Management for Remoting.....................286
   Using Remoting Across Multiple Systems...............287

Managing Cloud Resources with PowerShell.................288
   Managing Cloud Resources with PowerShell Modules. 288
   Automating Cloud Infrastructure Tasks....................294
   Managing Cloud Networking....................................297
   Best Practices for Managing Cloud Resources with PowerShell...298

Building Custom PowerShell Modules............................299
   Creating Your Own Reusable PowerShell Modules 300
   Packaging and Distributing Custom Modules..........303
   Importing and Using Custom Modules.....................305

- Best Practices for Custom Modules 306
- Using PowerShell with APIs and Web Services 308
  - Working with REST APIs and JSON Data in PowerShell 309
  - Handling Responses in PowerShell 313
  - Advanced Usage: Handling Complex APIs 315

Chapter 9 320
Real-World Case Studies and Examples 320
- Case Study 1: Automating Daily IT Maintenance 320
  - The PowerShell Solution: 322
  - Results and Benefits: 324
- Case Study 2: Troubleshooting and Optimizing Server Performance 326
  - The PowerShell Solution: 327
  - Results and Benefits: 334
- Case Study 3: Managing Active Directory at Scale 335
  - The PowerShell Solution: 337
  - Results and Benefits: 343
- Case Study 4: Reporting and Auditing in a Corporate Environment 345
  - The PowerShell Solution: 347
  - Results and Benefits: 353

Chapter 10 356
Conclusion and Next Steps 356
- Summary of Key Takeaways 356
- How to Continue Your PowerShell Journey 360
- Encouragement to Experiment and Automate 362

Appendix 366
- A: PowerShell Cmdlet Reference 366
- B: PowerShell Error Handling 372

C: PowerShell Script Template.................................374
D: Troubleshooting PowerShell Scripts....................376
E: Useful PowerShell Resources.............................377
About the Author..380

Introduction

Picture this: it's late on a Friday afternoon, and your phone buzzes. A high-priority alert pops up—one of the core servers is about to run out of disk space, and a critical application is showing signs of failure. You know that if the situation isn't resolved immediately, it could trigger hours of downtime, affecting hundreds of employees, delaying projects, and potentially costing the company thousands of dollars.

But here's the kicker: You've seen this issue before. The team has already tried manual fixes several times, running diagnostics, checking logs, freeing up disk space—nothing seems to prevent the issue from happening again and again. You're exhausted, overwhelmed, and frustrated. The clock is ticking, and you know you can't afford to let this happen again.

So, what's the solution? You don't have time for a deep dive into new tools, but what if there was a way to automate these tasks, a way to make the server work *for you*, instead of constantly being on the defensive?

This is where *PowerShell* comes in.

What PowerShell Is and Why It's Essential

In the world of IT, PowerShell is nothing short of a game-changer. It's the Swiss army knife of system administration, capable of automating the mundane, fixing the unfixable, and ultimately transforming your workflow. From managing hundreds of servers at once, automating software deployments, to running real-time diagnostics, PowerShell empowers you to make complex tasks simple, to resolve issues at lightning speed, and to drive efficiency in a way that manual processes could never achieve.

PowerShell is more than just a scripting language. It's a powerful tool that allows you to interact with the very heart of your system, control and automate tasks that once required significant time and expertise, and help you avoid the frustration of dealing with repetitive issues. For the IT professional, system administrator, or anyone responsible for keeping systems running smoothly, PowerShell is a vital skill—one that will save you time, eliminate errors, and give you back precious hours in your day.

But let's be real: learning PowerShell can seem overwhelming at first. You're faced with a myriad of commands, syntaxes, and concepts that may feel like an impenetrable wall. And that's where this book comes in.

Why This Book?

"PowerShell Made Simple: Solve IT Challenges, Save Time, and Improve Operations" is not just another technical manual full of jargon or abstract theory. This is a hands-on guide designed to take you from confusion to clarity, step-by-step. Whether you're new to PowerShell or have dabbled with it in the past, this book will empower you to solve real-world IT challenges, streamline operations, and improve system performance with practical, actionable skills.

Every chapter of this book is designed with one goal in mind: to make you *the PowerShell expert your IT environment needs*. You'll learn how to automate routine tasks, troubleshoot servers more efficiently, manage Active Directory, generate reports, and monitor system performance—all through clear, easy-to-understand instructions. Even more importantly, you'll understand *why* you're doing these things, giving you the confidence to adapt and expand your PowerShell knowledge to fit your specific needs.

How This Book Works

We know that as an IT professional, your time is precious. You're not looking for fluff or filler. You want results—immediate, actionable, and scalable. That's why this book is structured to give you maximum impact without wasting your time.

Here's how it works:
- Step-by-Step Instructions: Each chapter provides clear instructions on how to execute the most essential PowerShell tasks. No guesswork—just proven techniques you can start using immediately.
- Hands-On Exercises: You'll apply what you learn with practical exercises, reinforcing your knowledge and building your confidence.
- Real-World Case Studies: You'll see how PowerShell is used in actual IT environments to solve common (and not-so-common) challenges. This helps you envision how PowerShell fits into your own operations and gives you inspiration for your next big automation project.
- Beginner to Advanced: Whether you're a complete beginner or someone with experience, this book caters to all levels. You'll start with foundational concepts and gradually move on to more advanced techniques as you build your skills. And if you're already experienced, you'll find plenty of advanced tricks and best practices to take your PowerShell game to the next level.
- Proven Tips and Techniques: Throughout the book, you'll find expert tips and tricks that will save you time and effort, help you avoid common pitfalls, and boost your productivity.

Target Audience: Who Should Read This Book?

This book is for anyone who works with IT systems—especially those who need to automate routine tasks, troubleshoot issues efficiently, or improve system performance. Whether you're a:

- System Administrator: Automate server management, configure networking, or simplify user administration.
- Network Engineer: Manage network devices, diagnose issues, and optimize your infrastructure.
- IT Operations Manager: Streamline repetitive tasks, monitor system health, and keep everything running smoothly.
- Security Administrator: Automate security checks, log analysis, and compliance audits.
- Tech Enthusiast: If you're just curious about automating your own personal projects or improving your tech skills, PowerShell will open doors you never knew existed.

This book will guide you through the essential PowerShell concepts you need to know, and it will show you exactly how to apply these skills in a real IT environment.

A Glimpse Into What's Coming

The first chapters will introduce you to the basics of PowerShell—understanding the syntax, how to run simple scripts, and how to perform key administrative tasks. But from there, we'll quickly dive into the real power of PowerShell: automation. You'll learn how to:
- Automate common IT tasks like creating user accounts, managing servers, and performing backups.
- Use PowerShell to troubleshoot and resolve server issues with lightning speed.
- Monitor system health, track performance, and generate reports to stay ahead of problems.
- Create custom scripts and tools that can save you hours each week, all while reducing errors and increasing system uptime.

Your PowerShell Journey Starts Here

By the end of this book, you won't just know *how* to use PowerShell—you'll understand *why* you're using it, how to adapt it to your unique needs, and how it can radically transform the way you work. Whether you're automating server management, troubleshooting network issues, or improving security, PowerShell is the ultimate tool to take your IT career—and your organization—to the next level.

So, are you ready to solve your IT challenges, save time, and improve your operations? Let's get started. Turn the page, and let's unlock the power of PowerShell together.

Chapter 1

Understanding PowerShell Fundamentals

In the ever-evolving landscape of IT, the ability to automate, troubleshoot, and manage systems efficiently is a game-changer. PowerShell, the powerful scripting language and command-line interface developed by Microsoft, offers exactly that. Whether you're a system administrator, network engineer, or IT professional, PowerShell is an indispensable tool in your arsenal. It not only simplifies complex administrative tasks but also gives you the ability to automate processes that would otherwise take hours to complete manually.

In this chapter, we'll lay the foundation for your PowerShell journey. We'll start by introducing the core concepts and components of PowerShell, so you can understand how it works and why it's so effective in IT environments. By the end of this chapter, you'll have a solid grasp of how to use PowerShell's command-line interface, run basic commands, and begin writing your first simple scripts. This chapter is designed for beginners, but even if you have some experience with

PowerShell, the principles covered here will help you solidify your knowledge and ensure you're building on a strong foundation.

What is PowerShell?

PowerShell is a powerful, task-based command-line interface and scripting language that was developed by Microsoft. It was first released in 2006 as an automation tool for system administrators, allowing them to automate the administration of Windows systems and perform complex tasks with ease. Built on the .NET framework, PowerShell combines the best features of traditional command-line tools with the power of object-oriented programming, making it uniquely suited for managing modern IT infrastructures.

Unlike other command-line tools, PowerShell allows users to work with *objects* rather than just text. This distinction is crucial because objects can contain more than just simple output—they hold properties and methods that can be manipulated and processed in complex ways. This object-oriented approach provides PowerShell with flexibility and depth, enabling users to not only execute commands but also to interact with the system in a more structured and powerful way.

A Brief History of PowerShell

PowerShell's journey began as a tool aimed at providing system administrators with more control over their Windows environments. Initially, the command-line experience for Windows was limited to the old *CMD* (Command Prompt), which lacked advanced automation features. In contrast, Bash on Linux systems offered more powerful scripting capabilities, but Windows administrators were left with few options for efficient task automation.

To address this gap, PowerShell was created to be a more advanced command-line tool that could do everything CMD and Bash could do—and more. With its release in 2006, PowerShell quickly became a crucial tool for Windows server administrators and IT professionals. It continued to evolve with frequent updates, eventually being made open-source in 2016 with the release of *PowerShell Core*, allowing it to run on Windows, Linux, and macOS.

PowerShell vs. Traditional Command-Line Tools (CMD, Bash)

While *CMD* and *Bash* are both command-line interfaces used for interacting with operating systems, PowerShell is distinct in several key ways:

1. Object-Oriented vs. Text-Based: The most significant difference is that PowerShell works with objects, while CMD and Bash work with plain text. This means that in PowerShell, you can pass around objects that contain both data and actions, which can be manipulated programmatically. In CMD and Bash, output is typically just text that has to be parsed manually.

2. Cmdlets vs. Commands: PowerShell uses cmdlets—small, single-function commands designed to perform specific tasks. These cmdlets are designed to be easily combined into scripts for automating complex processes. In contrast, CMD and Bash rely on simple commands that are typically less specialized and don't always support automation in the same way.

3. Cross-Platform Capabilities: PowerShell started as a Windows-only tool, but with PowerShell Core, it became cross-platform, allowing it to be used on Linux and macOS systems as well. CMD is exclusive to Windows, and Bash, though widely used on Linux and macOS, isn't available natively on Windows without tools like Windows Subsystem for Linux (WSL).

4. Integration with .NET: PowerShell has deep integration with the .NET framework, allowing users to access and manipulate .NET libraries directly from the command line. This is a major advantage over CMD and Bash, which do not offer such robust integration with system-level programming libraries.

In summary, PowerShell stands out as a comprehensive, object-oriented automation tool that goes far beyond the capabilities of traditional command-line tools like CMD and Bash. It provides system administrators with powerful, flexible scripting tools to manage and automate tasks, making it an essential tool for modern IT operations.

PowerShell Syntax Basics

PowerShell's syntax is designed to be intuitive and flexible, combining traditional command-line elements with powerful scripting capabilities. To get started with PowerShell, it's important to understand some of its core concepts and building blocks: cmdlets, pipelines, and objects. Additionally, PowerShell has its own set of shortcuts and structures, such as aliases, parameters, and variables, that help make scripting faster and more efficient.

Cmdlets

Cmdlets (pronounced *"command-lets"*) are the fundamental building blocks of PowerShell. These are specialized commands that perform a specific task, and they are designed to be simple, focused, and easy to use. Cmdlets follow a consistent *Verb-Noun* naming convention, where the verb describes the action (such as *Get*, *Set*, *New*, or *Remove*) and the noun describes the object being acted upon (such as *Process*, *Service*, or *Item*). For example:

- `Get-Process`: Retrieves information about running processes on the system.
- `Set-Item`: Modifies an item, like a file or registry key.
- `New-User`: Creates a new user account.

This predictable structure makes it easier to remember and use PowerShell cmdlets.

Pipelines

One of PowerShell's most powerful features is the *pipeline*. A pipeline allows you to chain cmdlets together, passing the output of one cmdlet as the input to the next. This is where PowerShell's object-oriented nature becomes particularly useful—because it passes objects (not just text) through the pipeline, enabling more complex operations to be performed seamlessly.

For example, if you wanted to list all running processes and filter them by name, you could use the following command:

```powershell
Get-Process | Where-Object { $_.Name -like "chrome" }
```

Here, the `Get-Process` cmdlet retrieves all running processes, and the `Where-Object` cmdlet filters them by the process name. The pipe symbol (`|`) connects these two cmdlets, allowing you to work with the data as objects rather than simple text.

Objects

In PowerShell, everything is an *object*. This is a major difference between PowerShell and traditional command-line interfaces, which often treat everything as a string of text. Objects can contain properties (such as a process's memory usage) and methods (such as actions that can be performed on a file). This object-oriented approach makes it easier to manipulate data in sophisticated ways.

For instance, when using `Get-Process`, the output is an object that contains various properties such as `CPU`, `Memory`, and `Name`. You can easily access these properties using dot notation:

```powershell
(Get-Process "chrome").CPU
```

This will return the CPU time used by the Chrome process. By working with objects, PowerShell allows for a more structured and flexible approach to managing and automating tasks.

Aliases

PowerShell also provides *aliases* for cmdlets, which are shorthand names that are easier to type but perform the same tasks as their full cmdlet names. For example:

- `ls` is an alias for `Get-ChildItem`
- `cp` is an alias for `Copy-Item`
- `rm` is an alias for `Remove-Item`

Aliases are especially useful when working interactively in the PowerShell console, as they can save time and reduce the amount of typing needed.

Parameters

Cmdlets often accept *parameters* that modify their behavior or specify additional input. Parameters can be optional or mandatory, and they are usually specified after the cmdlet name using a `-` followed by the parameter name. For example:

```powershell
Get-Process -Name "chrome"
```

In this case, the `-Name` parameter specifies that you want to retrieve information about the "chrome" process. Parameters allow you to customize the behavior of cmdlets and make your scripts more flexible.

Variables

In PowerShell, *variables* are used to store data so it can be used later. Variables are denoted by a dollar sign (`$`), followed by the variable name. For example:

```powershell
$processName = "chrome"
Get-Process         -Name $processName
```

In this case, the variable `$processName` stores the string `"chrome"`, which is then used as input for the `Get-Process` cmdlet. Variables make it easy to store and reuse information in your scripts.

By mastering these core components—cmdlets, pipelines, objects, aliases, parameters, and variables—you'll be well on your way to writing efficient and powerful PowerShell scripts. Each of these elements plays a vital role in how PowerShell operates and interacts with your system, making it a flexible tool for automating IT tasks and managing your environment.

PowerShell Environment

Understanding the PowerShell environment is key to becoming proficient with the tool. PowerShell offers two primary interfaces for working with scripts and commands: the *PowerShell Console* and the *Integrated Scripting Environment (ISE)*. Both of these tools serve different purposes and provide distinct user experiences, but they share the same underlying functionality.

PowerShell Console vs. Integrated Scripting Environment (ISE)

- PowerShell Console: The PowerShell Console is the traditional command-line interface where you can run PowerShell commands interactively. It's a straightforward interface where you type one command at a time, and the output is immediately displayed. It's excellent for quick, one-off tasks or troubleshooting, as it allows you to execute commands and receive immediate feedback. However, the console lacks some of the advanced features that can enhance productivity in more complex scripting tasks.

- PowerShell ISE: The PowerShell Integrated Scripting Environment (ISE) is a more feature-rich interface, designed for writing and debugging scripts. It provides a graphical user interface (GUI) with several features not available in the console, such as:

- Syntax highlighting, which makes the script easier to read.
- Code completion, which helps reduce errors and speeds up script writing.
- A script editor where you can write, test, and debug larger scripts with multiple lines of code.
- The ability to run scripts and commands in separate panes, making it easier to organize your work.

The ISE is more suited for development and debugging of complex scripts, whereas the console is better for running individual commands quickly. If you're working on long scripts or managing automation tasks, the ISE provides a more comfortable, efficient environment. However, for quick, on-the-go tasks, the PowerShell console remains an effective choice.

Setting Up and Customizing PowerShell

PowerShell can be customized to fit your specific needs and workflow. Here are some common ways to set up and personalize your PowerShell environment:

1. Profiles: PowerShell profiles allow you to configure the environment every time PowerShell starts. This can include setting up default variables, custom functions, importing modules, or changing the prompt appearance. The profile is a script file that PowerShell runs automatically on startup, and there are different profiles for the console and ISE.

   - To find or create a profile, you can use the `$PROFILE` variable:

```powershell
notepad $PROFILE
```

   - This opens the profile script in Notepad, where you can add your custom configurations.

2. Changing the Prompt: You can customize the prompt to display useful information or just for aesthetic reasons. For example, you can modify the prompt to show the current directory, time, or even a custom message.

To change the prompt in the console or ISE:

```powershell
function prompt {
"MyCustomPrompt> " }
```

3. Color Customization: PowerShell allows you to adjust the color scheme of the text in the console. You can change the colors for output, errors, warnings, and more. This helps improve visibility, especially when running scripts with lots of output.

For example, to change the background color to black and text color to green:

```powershell
$Host.UI.RawUI.BackgroundColor = "Black"
$Host.UI.RawUI.ForegroundColor = "Green"
Clear-Host
```

4. Modules and Snap-ins: PowerShell's functionality can be extended through modules and snap-ins, which

provide additional cmdlets and functions. You can load these modules into your session to add tools for managing specific technologies like Active Directory, SQL Server, or Azure.

To load a module:

```powershell
Import-Module "ModuleName"
```

5. Aliases and Functions: PowerShell allows you to define your own aliases for frequently used cmdlets or create functions for more complex or repetitive tasks. Custom functions save you time and simplify your scripts.

For example, creating a function to list all running services:

```powershell
function Get-RunningServices {
    Get-Service | Where-Object {$_.Status -eq 'Running'}
}
```

6. Execution Policy: By default, PowerShell has an execution policy that restricts the running of scripts for security purposes. You can adjust this policy to suit your needs, especially if you are working with automation scripts that need to be executed.

To check the current execution policy:

```powershell
Get-ExecutionPolicy
```

To change the policy (e.g., to allow all scripts to run):

```
powershell

Set-ExecutionPolicy RemoteSigned
```

By understanding the differences between the PowerShell Console and ISE, as well as how to customize your PowerShell environment, you can tailor your experience to be more efficient, user-friendly, and suited to your specific needs. This flexibility is one of the reasons why PowerShell is such a powerful tool for IT professionals, system administrators, and anyone looking to streamline their workflow through automation and scripting.

Introduction to PowerShell Scripting

PowerShell scripting is the foundation for automating tasks, managing IT infrastructure, and streamlining operations. This section introduces the essential concepts of writing and running PowerShell scripts, along with error handling and debugging techniques to ensure your scripts perform smoothly.

Writing Basic Scripts and Running Them

PowerShell scripts are collections of commands and instructions that are executed sequentially. Scripts allow you to automate repetitive tasks, manage systems, and configure networks with ease. Writing your first PowerShell script is simple and follows basic principles:

1. Creating a Script: PowerShell scripts are saved with the `.ps1` extension. You can write scripts using a text editor (such as Notepad or Visual Studio Code) or directly in the PowerShell Integrated Scripting Environment (ISE).
   - To create a new script, open a text editor and save the file with the `.ps1` extension.

2. Basic Script Example: A simple PowerShell script might look like this:

```powershell
# This is a comment
$name = "John"
    Write-Host "Hello, $name"
```

In this script:
   - `$name` is a *variable* storing the string `"John"`.

- `Write-Host` is used to display output to the console.
- The `#` symbol is used to add comments that do not affect the script's functionality.

3. Running the Script: To execute a PowerShell script, simply type the script's path in the PowerShell console. For example:

```powershell
C:\Path\To\Script\example.ps1
```

If you're working in the ISE, you can press *F5* to run the script directly.

Note: If you encounter issues with script execution, it could be due to PowerShell's execution policy (which restricts the running of scripts for security reasons). To change this policy, run:

```powershell
    Set-ExecutionPolicy RemoteSigned
```

Error Handling and Debugging Basics

While scripting in PowerShell, errors are inevitable. Whether it's a syntax error, an unexpected result, or an environmental issue, knowing how to handle and troubleshoot errors is essential for writing robust scripts.

1. Basic Error Handling:
   - PowerShell provides an in-built *try-catch-finally* block to handle errors effectively.
   - The *try* block contains code that might throw an error.
   - The *catch* block contains the actions to take if an error occurs.
   - The *finally* block is optional and runs after the try-catch, regardless of whether an error occurred.

   Example of error handling:

```powershell
try {
    # Try to divide by zero
    $result = 10 / 0
}
catch {
    Write-Host "Error occurred: $_"
}
finally {
    Write-Host "This always runs"
}
```

In this example, dividing by zero triggers an error, which is caught by the catch block, displaying a custom message. The finally block runs regardless of whether the error was caught.

2. Checking for Errors Using `$Error`:

After running a command, you can examine the `$Error` variable, which holds the last error that occurred.

```powershell
$Error[0]    # Displays the most recent error
```

3. Throwing Custom Errors:
Sometimes, you may want to raise a custom error. This can be done using the `throw` keyword, which triggers an exception.

```powershell
if ($name -eq "") {
    throw "Name cannot be empty"
}
```

If `$name` is empty, the script will throw a custom error message.

4. Debugging:
PowerShell offers debugging features that allow you to step through your script to identify the root cause of issues.

- Use the `Set-PSDebug -Step` command to enable step-by-step debugging.

- Use `Write-Host` or `Write-Debug` to display information during script execution.

Example:
```powershell
Write-Debug "Checking variable $name"
```

To enable debugging output, you can run:
```powershell
$DebugPreference = "Continue"
```

5. Common Errors and Solutions:
- Syntax Errors: Often caused by missing parentheses, curly braces, or commas. Ensure your code is well-formed.
- Variable Errors: Ensure variables are properly defined and initialized before use.
- Permission Issues: Make sure that your script has the necessary permissions to execute

commands, especially when accessing system resources.

Mastering PowerShell scripting is about more than just writing code—it's about understanding the common pitfalls and having the tools to troubleshoot and debug your scripts when something goes wrong. In this chapter, you've learned how to create basic scripts, run them, and handle errors effectively. These fundamental skills are the building blocks for creating more complex and efficient PowerShell automation solutions.

Mastering PowerShell begins with understanding its fundamentals. By now, you should be familiar with the PowerShell environment, its essential components, and how to execute commands to perform basic administrative tasks. With this knowledge, you're ready to start automating tasks, troubleshooting issues, and improving system management.

The core concepts you've learned in this chapter will serve as the building blocks for more advanced topics. From here, we will dive deeper into PowerShell's full potential, exploring ways to automate complex workflows, manage systems at scale, and even troubleshoot and optimize performance. PowerShell's flexibility is its greatest strength, and understanding its fundamentals will allow you to harness that power to solve real-world IT challenges.

In the next chapter, we'll begin working with more complex scripts, functions, and automation techniques, empowering you to create robust solutions that save you time and increase operational efficiency. You're well on your way to becoming a PowerShell pro—let's keep building!

Chapter 2

PowerShell Core Concepts and Language Features

In this chapter, we will delve deeper into the core concepts and language features that form the foundation of PowerShell. Understanding these elements is essential for unlocking the full potential of PowerShell, whether you're automating routine tasks, managing systems, or developing complex scripts. From variables and data types to the powerful concepts of cmdlets and pipelines, this chapter will provide you with the knowledge needed to write efficient, scalable, and maintainable PowerShell code. By the end, you'll be well-equipped to handle a wide variety of IT automation tasks and to troubleshoot, optimize, and extend your scripts effectively.

Variables and Data Types

PowerShell, like any programming language, uses variables to store data that can be accessed and manipulated throughout the script. Understanding how to declare and work with variables, along with grasping the key data types available in PowerShell, is essential for writing effective scripts.

How to Declare and Use Variables

In PowerShell, variables are created by using a dollar sign (`$`) followed by the variable name. A variable can store data of any type, whether it's a string, number, or more complex data structure like an array or hashtable. The basic syntax to declare a variable is:

```powershell
$variableName = value
```

For example:

```powershell
$name = "John Doe"
$age = 30
```

In this case, `$name` is a variable that stores a string value `"John Doe"`, and `$age` is a variable that holds an integer value `30`.

PowerShell also has the ability to dynamically type variables, which means you don't need to explicitly declare the type (e.g., String, Integer). PowerShell will automatically assign the appropriate type based on the value assigned to the variable.

Key Data Types

PowerShell supports several key data types that allow you to store and manipulate a wide range of data:

1. String

A string is a sequence of characters. It is one of the most commonly used data types in PowerShell. Strings are declared using either single (`'`) or double (`"`) quotes.

Example:

```powershell
$name = "Alice"
$message = 'Hello, World!'
```

Strings are often used to represent text and can include spaces, special characters, and variables. When using double quotes, PowerShell also allows for variable interpolation:

```powershell
$greeting = "Hello, $name"
```

This would output: `Hello, Alice`.

2. Integer

Integers represent whole numbers. PowerShell does not require explicit data type definitions for integers, but you can use specific types like `[int]` for integers when you want to enforce type safety.

Example:

```powershell
$age = 25
$sum = 5 + 10
```

3. Array

An array is a collection of items stored in a single variable. Arrays allow you to group multiple values together, whether those values are of the same type or not. Arrays are particularly useful when you need to work with lists of data, such as file names, user names, or other objects.

Example:

```powershell
$fruits = @("Apple", "Banana", "Cherry")
```

Arrays can be accessed by their index, starting from `0`. For example, `$fruits[0]` would return `"Apple"`.

4. Hashtable

A hashtable is a collection of key-value pairs, often used to represent objects with properties. Each key in a hashtable is unique and maps to a value, making hashtables a great way to manage related data. You can create a hashtable by using the `@{}` syntax.

Example:

```powershell
$person = @{
    Name = "John Doe"
    Age = 30
    Location = "New York"
}
```

In this case, `$person` is a hashtable that stores a name, age, and location as key-value pairs. You can access individual values by referencing the key:

```powershell
$person["Name"]   # Outputs: John Doe
```

Type Conversion

PowerShell also supports type conversion, where you can explicitly convert between different data types. This can be useful when you're working with user input or dealing with data that comes from various sources, such as files, databases, or other scripts.

Example:

```powershell
$numberString = "123"
$number = [int]$numberString   # Converts the string "123" to an integer
```

Understanding how to declare and use variables, as well as the different data types in PowerShell, is a critical part of mastering the language. With these fundamentals in place, you'll be able to manipulate and store data efficiently, which is key to creating powerful, dynamic scripts. As you continue learning, these concepts will form the backbone of the automation tasks you undertake, from simple scripts to complex IT solutions.

Control Flow and Logic

Control flow and logic are essential for directing the execution of your PowerShell scripts. By using conditional statements, loops, and error handling, you can create dynamic and flexible scripts that respond to different scenarios and data inputs. These tools allow you to implement decision-making processes, repeat actions, and handle errors gracefully, ensuring your scripts work reliably in various situations.

Conditional Statements (if, else, switch)

Conditional statements allow your script to make decisions based on certain conditions. These conditions are evaluated as either `True` or `False`, and depending on the result, the script will execute specific blocks of code.

1. if...else Statement

The `if` statement is used to evaluate a condition. If the condition is true, the associated block of code runs. If the condition is false, an optional `else` block can be executed.

Example:

```powershell
$age = 18

if ($age -ge 18) {
    Write-Host "You are an adult."
} else {
        Write-Host "You are not an adult."
}
```

In this example, the script checks if the variable `$age` is greater than or equal to 18. If so, it prints `"You are an adult."` Otherwise, it prints `"You are not an adult."`

2. switch Statement

The `switch` statement is used when you need to compare a single value against multiple possible conditions. It's useful for handling more complex decision-making processes without writing multiple `if` conditions.

Example:

```powershell
$day = "Monday"

switch ($day) {
    "Monday" { Write-Host "Start of the week" }
    "Friday" { Write-Host "End of the week" }
    "Saturday" { Write-Host "Weekend!" }
    default { Write-Host "Another day" }
}
```

In this case, `$day` is evaluated against multiple possible values. The script prints the corresponding message depending on the value of `$day`. If none of the conditions match, the `default` case is executed.

Loops (for, foreach, while)

Loops are used to repeatedly execute a block of code until a specified condition is met. They are invaluable for performing repetitive tasks, such as processing a list of files or iterating through multiple items.

1. for Loop

The `for` loop is used when you know how many times you need to repeat a block of code. It consists of three parts: initialization, condition, and increment.

Example:

```powershell
for ($i = 0; $i -lt 5; $i++) {
    Write-Host "Iteration number: $i"
}
```

In this example, the loop starts with `$i = 0` and continues until `$i` is less than 5. After each iteration, `$i` is incremented by 1.

2. foreach Loop

The `foreach` loop is used to iterate over each element in a collection, such as an array, list, or even the output of a command.

Example:

```powershell
$fruits = @("Apple", "Banana", "Cherry")

foreach ($fruit in $fruits) {
  Write-Host "Fruit: $fruit"
}
```

Here, the script loops through each element in the `$fruits` array and prints out the name of each fruit.

3. while Loop

The `while` loop is used when you want to execute a block of code as long as a certain condition is true.

Example:

```powershell
$count = 0

while ($count -lt 5) {
        Write-Host "Count is $count"
    $count++
}
```

In this example, the loop runs until `$count` reaches 5. The value of `$count` is incremented after each iteration.

Error Handling (try/catch/finally)

Error handling is an important part of writing robust PowerShell scripts. The `try`, `catch`, and `finally` blocks allow you to handle exceptions (errors) that may occur during script execution. This prevents the script from crashing and allows you to provide meaningful feedback or recovery actions.

1. try Block

The `try` block is used to enclose code that might generate an error. If an error occurs, the script will jump to the `catch` block.

Example:

```powershell
try {
    $result = 10 / 0  # Division by zero
}
catch {
         Write-Host "An error occurred: $_"
}
```

In this case, dividing by zero will trigger an error, and the message `"An error occurred: $_"` will be printed.

2. catch Block

The `catch` block is used to handle the error. The `$_` variable represents the error message or exception details.

Example:

```powershell
try {
    $result = 10 / 0  # Division by zero
}
catch {
    Write-Host "Error: $_. Message: $($_.Exception.Message)"
}
```

This provides more detailed error information, including the specific exception message.

3. finally Block

The `finally` block is optional and contains code that will run whether an error occurred or not. It's often used to perform cleanup operations, such as closing files or releasing resources.

Example:

```powershell
try {
    $file = Get-Content "C:\path\to\file.txt"
}
catch {
    Write-Host "Could not read the file."
}
finally {
    Write-Host "Cleanup completed."
}
```

Here, even if an error occurs while reading the file, the `finally` block will execute and print `"Cleanup completed."`

Mastering control flow, logic, and error handling in PowerShell is crucial for creating flexible, dynamic scripts that can adapt to different scenarios. Whether you're working with simple conditions or looping through large datasets, understanding how to implement conditional logic and handle errors gracefully will significantly improve the reliability and effectiveness of your scripts. As you continue to build more complex automation tasks, these concepts will allow you to respond to varying inputs, make intelligent decisions, and ensure that your scripts execute smoothly under different conditions.

Working with Objects

In PowerShell, everything is an object. Understanding how to work with objects, their properties, and their methods is crucial to leveraging PowerShell's full potential. Whether you're querying system information, managing files, or automating tasks, objects play a central role in how you interact with data and the environment. This section covers the fundamentals of working with objects and tools that help you explore and manipulate them.

Understanding Objects, Properties, and Methods

1. What is an Object?

An object is an instance of a class in PowerShell, and it represents a real-world entity or concept—such as a process, file, or system service. Objects are fundamental to PowerShell, and they encapsulate both data and functionality.

For example, when you use the `Get-Process` cmdlet, PowerShell returns a list of process objects that represent the running applications or tasks on the system. Each process object contains various properties (such as `Name`, `Id`, and `CPU`) and methods (such as `Kill()` for stopping the process).

2. Properties of Objects

Properties are attributes that define the characteristics of an object. These properties hold values that describe the object. For instance, the `FileInfo` object has properties such as `Name`, `Length`, and `CreationTime`.

Example:

```powershell
$file = Get-Item "C:\path\to\file.txt"
$file.Name          # Returns the name of the file
$file.Length        # Returns the size of the file in bytes
$file.CreationTime  # Returns the file's creation time
```

In this example, the `$file` object represents a file, and we can access its properties (e.g., `Name`, `Length`, `CreationTime`) to gather information about the file.

3. Methods of Objects

Methods are actions that objects can perform. They define behaviors or operations that can be executed on the object. For example, the `Process` object has a `Kill()` method that can be called to terminate a running process.

Example:

```powershell
$process = Get-Process "notepad"
$process.Kill()  # Terminates the Notepad process
```

Here, the `Kill()` method is used to terminate the `Notepad` process. Methods like this can perform operations such as starting, stopping, or manipulating the object in other ways.

Using `Get-Help`, `Get-Command`, and `Get-Member` to Explore Objects

PowerShell provides several tools that allow you to explore and interact with objects more effectively. These cmdlets help you discover information about available cmdlets, their parameters, and the members (properties and methods) of objects.

1. **`Get-Help`**

The `Get-Help` cmdlet provides documentation for cmdlets, functions, workflows, and scripts. It is useful for exploring what an object or cmdlet can do and understanding its syntax.

Example:

```powershell
Get-Help Get-Process
```

This command retrieves the help documentation for the `Get-Process` cmdlet. You can use `Get-Help` to learn about available parameters, usage examples, and descriptions of cmdlet behavior.

2. `Get-Command`

`Get-Command` is used to discover cmdlets, functions, workflows, or scripts available in the current session. It's particularly helpful when you are unsure of the exact cmdlet name or want to explore related cmdlets.

Example:

```powershell
Get-Command -Name *Process*
```

This command lists all cmdlets, functions, and scripts related to processes. The `Process` wildcard allows you to find cmdlets related to processes, such as `Get-Process`, `Stop-Process`, etc.

3. `Get-Member`

`Get-Member` allows you to explore the properties and methods of an object. It provides a list of members (properties, methods, and other members) of the object you are working with.

Example:

```powershell
$process = Get-Process "notepad"
$process | Get-Member
```

This command pipes the `$process` object to `Get-Member`, which then outputs a list of the properties and methods available for that object. For example, the `Get-Member` output might show properties like `Name`, `Id`, and methods like `Kill()`.

You can also filter the output of `Get-Member` to show only specific types of members (e.g., only methods or properties) using the `-MemberType` parameter.

Example:

```powershell
$process | Get-Member -MemberType Method
```

This would show only the methods available for the `Process` object, such as `Kill()`, `Start()`, and so on.

Practical Example: Exploring a File Object

Let's put these concepts into practice with a file object. We'll use the `Get-Item` cmdlet to retrieve a file object and explore its properties and methods using the tools mentioned above.

```powershell
# Get file object
$file = Get-Item "C:\path\to\file.txt"

# Get properties of the file
$file | Get-Member -MemberType Property

# Get methods of the file object
$file | Get-Member -MemberType Method

# Retrieve specific properties
$file.Name
$file.Length
$file.CreationTime

# Perform a method
$file.Delete() # Deletes the file
```

In this example, the `$file` object represents a file. We use `Get-Member` to explore its properties and methods. You can retrieve properties like `Name`, `Length`, and `CreationTime`, or invoke methods like `Delete()` to delete the file.

Understanding objects, their properties, and methods is a core skill in PowerShell. By leveraging the `Get-Help`, `Get-Command`, and `Get-Member` cmdlets, you can quickly explore and interact with objects, making your automation tasks more powerful and flexible. Mastering these tools allows you to build scripts that manipulate and manage resources in your environment with ease, whether you're working with files, processes, or system settings. As you continue working with PowerShell, the ability to explore and manipulate objects will be indispensable for writing efficient, effective scripts.

Creating and Using Functions

Functions are one of the most powerful features in PowerShell, allowing you to define reusable blocks of code that can be invoked whenever needed. By organizing your script into functions, you can improve code readability, reusability, and maintainability. In this section, we'll explore how to create and use functions in PowerShell, including defining parameters, working with return values, and adhering to best practices for creating clean and efficient functions.

Syntax and Best Practices for Defining Reusable Functions

In PowerShell, a function is defined using the `function` keyword, followed by the function's name and a block of code enclosed in curly braces `{}`. A function can accept parameters, perform actions, and return values.

Basic Syntax of a PowerShell Function:

```powershell
function FunctionName
{
    # Function body
    # Code to execute
}
```

For example, let's create a simple function that outputs a greeting message:

```powershell
function Greet-User {
    Write-Output "Hello, PowerShell User!"
}
```

To execute this function, you would simply call it by its name:

```powershell
Greet-User
```

This will output: `Hello, PowerShell User!`

Best Practices for Defining Functions:

1. Function Naming:
- Name your functions clearly and consistently. Follow a verb-noun convention, such as `Get-Data`, `Set-Config`, or `Update-Record`, to make the function's purpose immediately clear.
- Use a hyphen (`-`) to separate the verb and noun, making it easier to read and understand.

2. Keep Functions Small:
- A function should do one thing, and do it well. Keeping functions small and focused improves readability and makes it easier to maintain your scripts.
- If a function becomes too large, consider breaking it into smaller sub-functions.

3. Write Clear and Descriptive Comments:
  - Include comments at the beginning of the function to describe what it does, what parameters it accepts, and what it returns. This makes it easier for others (and your future self) to understand and use the function.

Example:

```powershell
function Get-UserInfo {
    <#
    This function retrieves information about a user.
    Parameters:
        - UserName (string): The username to search for.
    Returns:
        - A user object containing information about the user.
    #>
    # Function code here
}
```

4. *Return Early:*
   - If a function needs to exit early (e.g., due to an error or specific condition), return the result or exit immediately to prevent unnecessary processing.

Function Parameters and Return Values

Functions in PowerShell can accept parameters, allowing you to pass in values when calling the function. This makes your functions more flexible and reusable.

Additionally, functions can return values to provide feedback to the caller or to be used in further processing.

Defining Function Parameters:

You define parameters within the parentheses `()` after the function name. Parameters can be mandatory or optional, and you can assign default values to optional parameters.

Basic Example of a Function with Parameters:

```powershell
function Greet-User {
    param (
        [string]$UserName
    )
        Write-Output "Hello, $UserName!"
}
```

In this example, the `Greet-User` function accepts one parameter, `$UserName`. You can call this function and pass a value for the parameter:

74

```powershell
Greet-User -UserName "Alice"
```

This will output: `Hello, Alice!`

Using Optional Parameters with Default Values:

You can make parameters optional by providing default values. If the caller does not provide a value for the parameter, the function uses the default value.

```powershell
function Greet-User {
  param (
    [string]$UserName = "Guest"  # Default value if no username is provided
  )
          Write-Output "Hello, $UserName!"
}
```

Calling this function without any parameters will use the default value `Guest`:

```powershell
Greet-User
```

This will output: `Hello, Guest!`

Return Values from Functions:

By default, PowerShell functions return the output of the last statement executed in the function. You can also use the `return` keyword to explicitly return a value.

Example of a Function with Return Values:

```powershell
function Add-Numbers {
    param (
        [int]$Number1,
        [int]$Number2
    )
    $sum = $Number1 + $Number2
    return $sum
}
```

In this example, the `Add-Numbers` function returns the sum of two numbers. You can capture the return value by assigning the function call to a variable:

```powershell
$result = Add-Numbers -Number1 5 -Number2 7
Write-Output "The result is: $result"
```

This will output: `The result is: 12`

Alternatively, you can let PowerShell return the value automatically without using the `return` keyword:

```powershell
function Add-Numbers {
  param (
    [int]$Number1,
    [int]$Number2
  )
     $Number1 + $Number2   # PowerShell will return the result of this expression
}
```

Function Scope and Variables

Variables in functions have their scope, which refers to where they are accessible. By default, variables declared inside a function are local to that function and cannot be accessed outside of it. This helps to avoid conflicts between variables in different functions.

Example:

```powershell
function MyFunction {
  $localVariable = "I am local"
  Write-Output $localVariable
}

MyFunction  # Outputs: I am local
Write-Output $localVariable   # This will cause an error because $localVariable is not accessible outside the function
```

If you need to use a variable across multiple functions, you can either pass it as a parameter or define it globally using the `$global` scope modifier (though this is generally discouraged due to potential side effects).

Best Practices for Working with Functions

1. **Use Clear and Intuitive Names:**
   - As with cmdlets, functions should have clear, descriptive names that make their purpose immediately understandable.

2. **Handle Errors Inside Functions:**

- When writing functions, consider adding error handling (e.g., `try/catch`) to gracefully manage issues and prevent the function from failing unexpectedly.

3. **Return Meaningful Data:**
    - Functions should return meaningful data that can be used by other parts of your script or pipeline. Avoid returning unnecessary data that can clutter the output.

4. **Keep Functions Modular:**
    - Each function should handle a single task. If a function is doing too much, it may be time to break it into smaller, more manageable parts.

5. **Use Parameter Validation:**
    - You can use validation attributes on parameters (e.g., `[ValidateNotNullOrEmpty]`) to ensure that users provide valid input when calling the function.

Functions are an essential tool in PowerShell, allowing you to encapsulate logic into reusable units of code that improve the modularity and maintainability of your scripts. By defining parameters, handling return values, and adhering to best practices, you can create efficient, flexible, and reliable functions that will help automate your IT tasks. Understanding how to create and use functions effectively is a cornerstone of becoming proficient with PowerShell, whether you're managing servers, automating repetitive tasks, or building complex automation workflows.

Having explored the fundamental concepts of PowerShell in this chapter, you should now have a solid understanding of the core language features that make PowerShell such a powerful tool for IT professionals. From the use of variables and data types to the intricacies of cmdlets, pipelines, and object handling, these concepts serve as the building blocks for more advanced scripting techniques. Mastering these core concepts will not only enhance your ability to write efficient scripts but also empower you to leverage PowerShell to its fullest potential. As you continue to explore deeper aspects of PowerShell, these foundational skills will prove invaluable in solving real-world IT challenges and optimizing your workflows.

Chapter 3

Automating IT Tasks with PowerShell

In today's fast-paced IT environment, automation is no longer just a luxury—it's a necessity. Manual, repetitive tasks consume valuable time and resources, making them an inefficient use of an IT professional's skills. PowerShell, with its robust scripting capabilities, is the key to unlocking powerful automation across IT operations. In this chapter, we will dive into the core concepts and practical techniques that will allow you to automate routine IT tasks. From managing system configurations to orchestrating workflows, PowerShell enables you to reduce human error, increase efficiency, and focus your efforts on more complex challenges. Whether you're looking to automate server maintenance, manage Active Directory users, or streamline software deployment, PowerShell can transform your approach to IT operations. By the end of this chapter, you will be equipped with the tools and knowledge to automate tasks with confidence, saving time and improving system reliability.

Managing Files and Directories with PowerShell

PowerShell is a powerful tool for automating file and directory management. Whether you are working on a small project or managing a vast network of servers, knowing how to efficiently handle files and directories can make your job much easier. In this section, we'll explore the essential file and directory operations that every IT professional needs to know, from basic file manipulation to more advanced directory management.

File Operations

PowerShell provides a suite of cmdlets specifically designed for file management. These cmdlets enable you to easily copy, move, and delete files—whether you're working locally or remotely. Let's go over some of the most commonly used cmdlets for handling files.

1. Copying Files (`Copy-Item`)

The `Copy-Item` cmdlet is used to copy files or directories from one location to another. You can also use it to copy items between local machines or across network shares.

Example:

```powershell
Copy-Item -Path "C:\Source\file.txt" -Destination "C:\Destination\file.txt"
```

This will copy the file `file.txt` from the source directory to the destination directory.

To copy an entire directory:

```powershell
Copy-Item -Path "C:\Source\Directory" -Destination "C:\Destination" -Recurse
```

The `-Recurse` flag ensures that all files and subdirectories within the directory are copied.

2. Moving Files (`Move-Item`)

The `Move-Item` cmdlet moves files and directories from one location to another. It's particularly useful for reorganizing files or directories.

Example:

```powershell
Move-Item -Path "C:\Source\file.txt" -Destination "C:\Destination\file.txt"
```

This moves `file.txt` from the source directory to the destination directory.

3. Deleting Files (`Remove-Item`)

The `Remove-Item` cmdlet is used to delete files and directories. Be cautious with this cmdlet, as it will permanently delete the items.

Example:

```powershell
Remove-Item -Path "C:\Destination\file.txt"
```

This deletes the file `file.txt` from the destination directory.

To delete an entire directory, use the `-Recurse` flag:

```powershell
Remove-Item -Path "C:\Destination\Directory" -Recurse
```

4. Renaming Files (`Rename-Item`)

PowerShell also allows you to rename files and directories using the `Rename-Item` cmdlet.

Example:

```powershell
Rename-Item -Path "C:\Source\oldname.txt" -NewName "newname.txt"
```

This changes the name of `oldname.txt` to `newname.txt` in the source directory.

Directory Management

Managing directories is just as important as managing files, and PowerShell offers several cmdlets to help you create, list, and remove directories with ease.

1. Creating Directories (`New-Item`)

The `New-Item` cmdlet is used to create new directories. If the directory already exists, you will receive an error unless you specify the `-Force` flag.

Example:

```powershell
New-Item -Path "C:\NewDirectory" -ItemType Directory
```

This will create a new directory called `NewDirectory` on the C drive.

2. Listing Directory Contents (`Get-ChildItem`)

The `Get-ChildItem` cmdlet lists the contents of a directory, including files and subdirectories. You can use this cmdlet to inspect the contents of a folder or to retrieve information about files within a directory.

Example:

```powershell
Get-ChildItem -Path "C:\Source"
```

This will list all the files and directories within `C:\Source`.

You can also use the `-Recurse` flag to list items in subdirectories:

```powershell
Get-ChildItem -Path "C:\Source" -Recurse
```

3. Removing Directories (`Remove-Item`)

To remove a directory, use the `Remove-Item` cmdlet. If the directory contains files or subdirectories, you must use the `-Recurse` flag to delete everything inside it.

Example:

```powershell
Remove-Item -Path "C:\Destination\OldDirectory" -Recurse
```

This command deletes the directory `OldDirectory` and all its contents.

4. Checking Directory Existence (`Test-Path`)

Before performing actions on directories, it's often useful to check if a directory exists. PowerShell's `Test-Path` cmdlet helps you verify whether a path exists.

Example:

```powershell
Test-Path -Path "C:\NewDirectory"
```

This will return `True` if `NewDirectory` exists, or `False` if it doesn't.

Advanced File Operations

Beyond the basics of file and directory management, PowerShell also supports more advanced file operations like filtering, searching, and manipulating file properties.

1. Finding Files with Specific Criteria (`Get-ChildItem` with Filters)

You can use `Get-ChildItem` with wildcards or filtering options to locate files that match certain criteria. This is useful when working with large sets of files.

Example:

```powershell
Get-ChildItem -Path "C:\Documents" -Filter "*.txt"
```

This will return all `.txt` files in the `C:\Documents` directory.

2. Changing File Properties (`Set-ItemProperty`)

PowerShell allows you to change file properties, such as attributes and timestamps.

Example:

```powershell
Set-ItemProperty -Path "C:\file.txt" -Name "IsReadOnly" -Value $true
```

This will make `file.txt` read-only.

PowerShell is an incredibly powerful tool for managing files and directories, providing you with the flexibility to automate your workflows and streamline everyday tasks. With the ability to copy, move, delete, and create both files and directories, PowerShell simplifies many of the most common operations that IT professionals face. Additionally, PowerShell's ability to manipulate file properties and find files based on complex criteria enhances its utility for more advanced file management tasks. By mastering these commands, you'll be able to handle all of your file and directory management needs with ease, reducing the time spent on manual processes and increasing efficiency. Whether you're automating server maintenance tasks or managing a network of computers, PowerShell is an invaluable tool for keeping your systems organized and running smoothly.

Working with the Windows Registry Using PowerShell

The Windows registry is a critical component of the operating system, storing configuration settings, options, and information for both the system and installed applications. As an IT professional, having the ability to interact with the registry programmatically can be incredibly useful. PowerShell provides a set of cmdlets to read from and write to the Windows registry, allowing you to automate many tasks related to system configuration and application management.

In this section, we'll explore how to access and manipulate the registry using PowerShell. You'll learn how to read values, modify keys, and perform common registry tasks with ease.

Reading from the Windows Registry

Reading values from the registry can be done using the `Get-ItemProperty` cmdlet, which allows you to query specific registry keys and retrieve the values stored within them. You can access registry keys using the `HKCU` (HKEY_CURRENT_USER) or `HKLM` (HKEY_LOCAL_MACHINE) root paths, which represent different portions of the registry.

1. Reading a Registry Key Value:

To read a registry key value, you specify the path to the registry key and use `Get-ItemProperty` to extract the value.

Example:

```powershell
Get-ItemProperty -Path "HKCU:\Software\Microsoft\Windows\CurrentVersion\Explorer" -Name "Shell Folders"
```

This command retrieves the value stored under the "Shell Folders" property for the specified path in the current user registry hive.

Output:
The output will display the value associated with the "Shell Folders" property, showing the folder paths for the user's profile.

2. Reading All Values from a Registry Key:

If you want to read all properties of a specific registry key, you can omit the `-Name` parameter and the command will return all values associated with that key.

Example:

```powershell
Get-ItemProperty -Path "HKCU:\Software\Microsoft\Windows\CurrentVersion\Explorer"
```

This will list all properties and their corresponding values under the specified registry key.

3. Listing Registry Keys:

Sometimes you might want to see the list of keys within a specific registry hive or subkey. You can use the `Get-ChildItem` cmdlet to list all subkeys.

Example:

```powershell
Get-ChildItem -Path "HKCU:\Software\Microsoft\Windows\CurrentVersion"
```

This lists all the registry subkeys located under the specified path.

Writing to the Windows Registry

Writing to the registry is just as easy with PowerShell. The `Set-ItemProperty` cmdlet is used to modify or add registry values. You can also create new registry keys using the `New-Item` cmdlet, and delete keys or values with `Remove-ItemProperty`.

1. Writing a New Value to the Registry:

You can use `Set-ItemProperty` to write a new value or update an existing value in the registry.

Example:

```powershell
Set-ItemProperty -Path "HKCU:\Software\MySoftware" -Name "InstallPath" -Value "C:\Program Files\MySoftware"
```

This will create or modify the "InstallPath" value in the specified registry key with the new path `"C:\Program Files\MySoftware"`.

2. Creating a New Registry Key:

To create a new registry key, use the `New-Item` cmdlet. You can then add values to the newly created key using `Set-ItemProperty`.

Example:

```powershell
New-Item -Path "HKCU:\Software\MySoftware"
Set-ItemProperty -Path "HKCU:\Software\MySoftware" -Name "InstallPath" -Value "C:\Program Files\MySoftware"
```

This sequence of commands first creates a new registry key under `HKCU:\Software\MySoftware` and then adds the "InstallPath" value.

3. Modifying Existing Registry Values:

If a value already exists in the registry and you want to change it, simply use `Set-ItemProperty` to overwrite the value.

Example:

```powershell
Set-ItemProperty -Path "HKCU:\Software\Microsoft\Windows\CurrentVersion\Explorer" -Name "Shell Folders" -Value "C:\NewFolder"
```

This will change the value of the "Shell Folders" property to `"C:\NewFolder"`.

4. Deleting a Registry Value:

To remove a specific registry value, use the `Remove-ItemProperty` cmdlet.

Example:

```powershell
Remove-ItemProperty -Path "HKCU:\Software\MySoftware" -Name "InstallPath"
```

This removes the "InstallPath" value from the registry.

5. Deleting a Registry Key:

If you want to delete a registry key entirely, use `Remove-Item`:

Example:

```powershell
Remove-Item -Path "HKCU:\Software\MySoftware" -Recurse
```

This command removes the entire `MySoftware` registry key, along with any subkeys or values it contains.

Common Registry Tasks with PowerShell

PowerShell provides a variety of cmdlets to interact with the registry, making it a versatile tool for system administrators and IT professionals. Here are a few common registry-related tasks you might encounter:

1. Backup Registry Keys:

PowerShell allows you to back up registry keys before making any changes. This is a crucial step for preventing accidental changes.

Example:

```powershell
Export-RegistryKey -Path "HKCU:\Software\MySoftware" -Destination "C:\Backup\MySoftware.reg"
```

2. Search for Registry Entries:

You may need to search for specific entries across your registry. Use `Get-ChildItem` with `-Recurse` to search through registry keys.

Example:

```powershell
Get-ChildItem -Path "HKCU:\Software" -Recurse | Where-Object { $_.Name -like "*MySoftware*" }
```

This command will search for any keys or values that contain "MySoftware" in their name.

3. Monitoring Registry Changes:

PowerShell can also help you monitor changes to the registry. Using the `Register-WmiEvent` cmdlet, you can track registry modifications in real-time.

Example:

```powershell
Register-WmiEvent -Class Win32_RegistryChangeEvent -Action { Write-Host "Registry change detected!" }
```

PowerShell makes interacting with the Windows registry simple and straightforward. Whether you're reading values, writing new entries, or deleting outdated keys, PowerShell's cmdlets offer flexibility and precision. Mastering these registry-related tasks enables IT professionals to automate system configurations, manage software settings, and troubleshoot issues effectively. By understanding and leveraging PowerShell's capabilities to manage the registry, you can ensure smoother system operations, maintain consistency across systems, and ultimately save time in your day-to-day IT management tasks. Whether you're automating repetitive tasks or making changes to improve system performance, PowerShell is an indispensable tool for working with the Windows registry.

Process and Service Management with PowerShell

Managing processes and services is a core responsibility for IT professionals, system administrators, and anyone tasked with maintaining the health and performance of Windows environments. PowerShell provides powerful cmdlets to interact with both running processes and services, enabling you to monitor, control, and automate key system functions.

This section will walk you through how to manage processes and services with PowerShell. You'll learn how to view and manipulate running processes, and control Windows services — actions that are essential for troubleshooting, performance optimization, and routine system management.

Viewing and Managing Running Processes

Processes are fundamental to the operation of any computer. Each running program or service is represented by a process, and managing them effectively is vital for maintaining system stability and performance.

1. Viewing Running Processes:

To see a list of all currently running processes, PowerShell provides the `Get-Process` cmdlet. This cmdlet returns detailed information about each process, such as its ID, name, CPU usage, memory usage, and more.

Example:

```powershell
Get-Process
```

This will display all running processes on the local machine.

Filtering Processes:

You can filter the processes by name, CPU usage, memory consumption, or other criteria. For example, to find all processes related to "chrome", you can use:

```powershell
Get-Process -Name "chrome"
```

2. Viewing Specific Process Details:

If you want detailed information about a specific process, you can pipe the output to `Select-Object` to show only the properties you're interested in. For example, to display memory and CPU usage for a process, use:

Example:

```powershell
Get-Process -Name "chrome" | Select-Object Name, CPU, WS
```

Here, `WS` refers to "Working Set", which indicates the amount of memory used by the process.

3. Stopping a Process:

To stop a running process, use the `Stop-Process` cmdlet. You can specify the process by its name or Process ID (PID).

Example:

```powershell
Stop-Process -Name "chrome"
```

This will stop all instances of Chrome running on the machine.

If you need to stop a process by its PID, use:

```powershell
Stop-Process -Id 1234
```

4. Starting a Process:

To start a new process, use the `Start-Process` cmdlet. You can specify the application you want to launch, along with any arguments or parameters it might require.

Example:

```powershell
Start-Process "notepad.exe"
```

If you need to launch a process with specific arguments, you can pass those as parameters. For instance, to open a file in Notepad:

```powershell
Start-Process "notepad.exe" -ArgumentList "C:\Users\Documents\example.txt"
```

5. Monitoring Process Performance:

For ongoing process performance monitoring, you can use `Get-Process` combined with `Out-File` or `Export-Csv` to save process information to a file for later analysis.

Example:

```powershell
Get-Process | Export-Csv -Path "C:\process_list.csv"
```

Managing Windows Services

Windows services are background processes that run independently of the user interface, providing essential functionality to the system. These services handle everything from networking and system maintenance to security and application support. Managing services is a critical skill for IT administrators.

1. Viewing Services:

You can view the status of services with the `Get-Service` cmdlet. This will display all services currently running on the machine.

Example:

```powershell
Get-Service
```

To view the status of a specific service, use the `-Name` parameter:

Example:
```powershell
Get-Service -Name "wuauserv"
```

This will display the status of the "Windows Update" service.

2. Starting and Stopping Services:

To start or stop a service, use the `Start-Service` and `Stop-Service` cmdlets, respectively. You can specify the service name or use its `ServiceName` property.

Start a Service:

```powershell
Start-Service -Name "wuauserv"
```

Stop a Service:

```powershell
Stop-Service -Name "wuauserv"
```

To forcefully stop a service, you can add the `-Force` flag:

Example:

```powershell
Stop-Service -Name "wuauserv" -Force
```

3. Restarting Services:

Sometimes, services can become unresponsive or may need a refresh to apply new configurations. You can restart a service using `Restart-Service`.

Example:

```powershell
Restart-Service -Name "wuauserv"
```

4. Changing Service Startup Type:

Services can have different startup types: Automatic, Manual, or Disabled. You can modify these settings with the `Set-Service` cmdlet.

Example:
To set a service to start automatically:

```powershell
Set-Service -Name "wuauserv" -StartupType Automatic
```

To disable a service:

```powershell
Set-Service -Name "wuauserv" -StartupType Disabled
```

5. Checking Service Dependencies:

Some services rely on others to function properly. To view the dependencies of a service, use the `Get-Service` cmdlet in conjunction with `Select-Object`.

Example:

```powershell
Get-Service -Name "wuauserv" | Select-Object -ExpandProperty DependentServices
```

This will list any services that depend on "Windows Update."

Common Service and Process Management Scenarios

Here are a few common scenarios where managing processes and services with PowerShell can save time and improve system performance:

1. Automating Service Restarts for Maintenance:
Regular maintenance of system services is crucial for keeping systems stable. PowerShell allows you to create scheduled tasks or scripts to restart services at specific intervals.

Example:

```powershell
Restart-Service -Name "wuauserv"
```

2. Monitoring Process Performance:
PowerShell can be used to continuously monitor processes for high CPU or memory usage, automatically restarting or killing processes that are consuming too many resources.

3. Automated Recovery of Failed Services:

If a critical service fails, you can use PowerShell to create an alert or automatically restart the service, reducing downtime.

Managing processes and services effectively is one of the foundational tasks for any system administrator. PowerShell's cmdlets for process and service management give you the flexibility and control to monitor, control, and automate these operations with ease. Whether you are troubleshooting performance issues, automating service restarts, or simply keeping your system running smoothly, PowerShell enables you to handle these tasks efficiently and reliably. By mastering process and service management with PowerShell, you can significantly improve your ability to maintain healthy, optimized Windows environments, and automate repetitive management tasks.

Working with Event Logs in PowerShell

Event logs are essential for monitoring system health, troubleshooting issues, and auditing activities on Windows systems. PowerShell provides robust tools for accessing, filtering, and creating event logs, making it easier to automate event log management and integrate it into your IT workflows.

In this section, we will explore how to work with event logs using PowerShell. You'll learn how to view and filter logs, search for specific events, and even create your own custom event logs. These tasks are indispensable for IT professionals who need to keep systems running smoothly and track down issues that arise.

Viewing Event Logs

Windows Event Logs store records of important system events, including application errors, security events, and system issues. PowerShell provides several cmdlets for interacting with these logs, allowing you to retrieve, analyze, and manipulate event log data.

1. Viewing All Event Logs:

The `Get-EventLog` cmdlet allows you to retrieve events from the Windows event log. By default, it pulls data from the "Application" log, but you can specify other logs such as "System", "Security", or custom logs.

Example:

```powershell
Get-EventLog -LogName Application
```

This command will display the events in the Application log. You can replace "Application" with other log names like "System" or "Security" to access different logs.

2. Filtering Event Logs:

Often, you only need to see events that meet certain criteria, such as a specific event ID, severity level, or time range. You can filter the event log results by specifying parameters such as `-EntryType`, `-EventId`, `-After`, and `-Before`.

Example 1:
Filter logs to show only error events:
```powershell
Get-EventLog -LogName System -EntryType Error
```

Example 2:
Retrieve events with a specific event ID (e.g., 1000 for application crashes):

```powershell
Get-EventLog -LogName Application -EventId 1000
```

Example 3:
Retrieve logs between two dates:

```powershell
Get-EventLog -LogName System -After "2024-01-01" -Before "2024-02-01"
```

3. Limiting the Number of Entries:

Sometimes, you may only need a snapshot of recent events rather than the entire log. Use the `-Newest` parameter to limit the number of entries returned.

Example:
Get the 10 most recent events from the Application log:

```powershell
Get-EventLog -LogName Application -Newest 10
```

4. Viewing Event Details:

The output from `Get-EventLog` provides basic information such as the event ID, date, and message. You can pipe the output to `Select-Object` or `Format-List` to view more detailed information.

Example:

```powershell
Get-EventLog -LogName System -Newest 5 | Format-List *
```

This will display all the properties of the most recent five events in the System log.

Creating Custom Event Logs

PowerShell not only allows you to interact with existing event logs, but it also gives you the capability to create custom event logs. Custom logs can be useful for tracking application-specific events or monitoring activities that aren't captured in the default logs.

1. Creating a Custom Event Log:

To create a new event log, use the `New-EventLog` cmdlet. This cmdlet requires you to specify the log name and the source of the events (e.g., an application name or service).

Example:

```powershell
New-EventLog -LogName "MyCustomLog" -Source "MyApplication"
```

This creates a custom event log called "MyCustomLog" and links it to the event source "MyApplication". You can specify any name you like for the log and source.

2. Writing to the Custom Event Log:

Once the custom event log is created, you can write entries to it using the `Write-EventLog` cmdlet. You will need to specify the log name, source, event ID, and the message.

Example:

```powershell
Write-EventLog -LogName "MyCustomLog" -Source "MyApplication" -EventId 1001 -Message "This is a test event."
```

This command writes an event with ID 1001 to the "MyCustomLog" log, with the message "This is a test event."

3. Writing Different Types of Events:

You can specify the event type (information, warning, or error) using the `-EntryType` parameter. This allows you to categorize the events based on their severity.

Example:
Write an informational message:

```powershell
Write-EventLog -LogName "MyCustomLog" -Source "MyApplication" -EventId 1002 -EntryType Information -Message "Operation completed successfully."
```

Write a warning message:

```powershell
Write-EventLog -LogName "MyCustomLog" -Source "MyApplication" -EventId 1003 -EntryType Warning -Message "Disk space running low."
```

Write an error message:

```powershell
Write-EventLog -LogName "MyCustomLog" -Source "MyApplication" -EventId 1004 -EntryType Error -Message "Application failed to start."
```

4. Removing Custom Event Logs:

If you no longer need a custom event log, you can delete it using the `Remove-EventLog` cmdlet.

Example:

```powershell
Remove-EventLog -LogName "MyCustomLog"
```

This command will remove the "MyCustomLog" event log.

Automating Event Log Monitoring

Automating event log monitoring is one of the key strengths of PowerShell. For example, you can create scripts that automatically search for specific events in the log files and take action based on certain conditions. This is especially useful for alerting or taking corrective actions when critical events occur.

1. Automated Event Log Alerts:

You can use PowerShell scripts in combination with Task Scheduler to monitor event logs in real time and send alerts if specific types of events occur.

Example:
Monitor event logs and send an email when a critical error is logged:

```powershell
$events = Get-EventLog -LogName Application -EntryType Error -Newest 10
foreach ($event in $events) {
  if ($event.EventId -eq 1000) {
    Send-MailMessage -From "admin@example.com" -To "it@company.com" -Subject "Critical Error" -Body "Error 1000 detected: $($event.Message)"
  }
}
```

2. Scheduled Task to Monitor Logs:

Use PowerShell scripts to automate regular checks for specific event types and trigger tasks based on the results.

Example:

```powershell
$scriptblock = {
    $events = Get-EventLog -LogName Application -EntryType Error -Newest 5
    foreach ($event in $events) {
        if ($event.EventId -eq 1234) {
            Restart-Service -Name "MyService"
        }
    }
}
Register-ScheduledTask -Action $scriptblock -Trigger (New-ScheduledTaskTrigger -AtStartup)
```

Event log management is an essential aspect of maintaining and troubleshooting Windows systems. With PowerShell, you have the flexibility to view, filter, and create event logs, providing you with the tools needed to monitor system activity and automate responses to critical events. By mastering event log management, you can not only stay on top of system health but also proactively address issues before they escalate into serious problems. Whether you are monitoring security events, tracking application errors, or creating custom logs to suit your organization's needs,

PowerShell gives you full control over event logging, enabling you to maintain efficient, secure, and optimized IT environments.

Task Scheduling and Automation with PowerShell

Task scheduling and automation are critical components for maintaining consistent IT operations, reducing manual intervention, and ensuring systems are properly managed. PowerShell provides powerful tools for interacting with Windows Task Scheduler, allowing you to automate repetitive tasks, run scripts at specific times, and integrate IT operations seamlessly into your broader automation workflows.

In this section, we'll explore how to schedule tasks using PowerShell, automate regular IT maintenance, and ensure that critical system management tasks are executed without manual input. Whether it's scheduling daily backups, running maintenance scripts, or sending out periodic reports, automating these tasks will save time, reduce human error, and improve system reliability.

Scheduling Tasks with Task Scheduler Using PowerShell

Windows Task Scheduler allows you to run tasks at specified times or under certain conditions, such as when the computer starts or when a user logs in. PowerShell provides cmdlets to interact with Task Scheduler, enabling you to create, configure, and manage scheduled tasks programmatically.

1. Creating a Basic Scheduled Task:

You can create a new scheduled task using the `New-ScheduledTask` cmdlet and then register it with Task Scheduler using `Register-ScheduledTask`.

Example:
This command creates a task that runs a PowerShell script every day at 8:00 AM.

```powershell
$action = New-ScheduledTaskAction -Execute "PowerShell.exe" -Argument "-File C:\Scripts\BackupScript.ps1"
$trigger = New-ScheduledTaskTrigger -Daily -At "8:00AM"
$task = New-ScheduledTask -Action $action -Trigger $trigger -Description "Daily Backup Task"
Register-ScheduledTask -TaskName "DailyBackup" -InputObject $task
```

Explanation:

- `New-ScheduledTaskAction`: Defines the action to be performed (running a PowerShell script).
- `New-ScheduledTaskTrigger`: Specifies when the task will run (daily at 8:00 AM).
- `Register-ScheduledTask`: Registers the task in Task Scheduler.

2. Scheduling Tasks with Specific Conditions:

You can also schedule tasks based on specific conditions, such as when the system is idle, or when the computer is on AC power. PowerShell allows you to set these conditions when creating or modifying tasks.

Example:

Schedule a task to run only if the computer is idle for at least 10 minutes:

```powershell
$action = New-ScheduledTaskAction -Execute "PowerShell.exe" -Argument "-File C:\Scripts\SystemCleanup.ps1"
$trigger = New-ScheduledTaskTrigger -AtStartup
$trigger.IdleSettings = New-ScheduledTaskIdleSettings -IdleDuration 00:10:00
$task = New-ScheduledTask -Action $action -Trigger $trigger -Description "System Cleanup on Idle"
Register-ScheduledTask -TaskName "SystemCleanup" -InputObject $task
```

This task will run the `SystemCleanup.ps1` script when the system has been idle for 10 minutes.

3. Running Tasks with Elevated Privileges:

Sometimes, tasks require elevated privileges to execute (e.g., running a backup or modifying system settings). To run a scheduled task with administrator privileges, you can set the `-RunLevel` parameter to "Highest" when creating the task.

Example:

Create a scheduled task to run a script as an administrator:

```powershell
$action = New-ScheduledTaskAction -Execute "PowerShell.exe" -Argument "-File C:\Scripts\UpdateSoftware.ps1"
$trigger = New-ScheduledTaskTrigger -AtStartup
$task = New-ScheduledTask -Action $action -Trigger $trigger -Description "Software Update"
Register-ScheduledTask -TaskName "SoftwareUpdate" -InputObject $task -RunLevel Highest
```

This task ensures that the script is run with elevated privileges.

Automating Regular IT Maintenance Tasks

One of the most powerful ways to use PowerShell and Task Scheduler together is by automating routine IT maintenance tasks. These tasks can include things like disk cleanup, software updates, log file rotation, system backups, or monitoring system health. By automating these tasks, you free up valuable time and ensure that essential system management operations happen regularly and consistently.

1. Automating System Backups:

Regular backups are essential for disaster recovery and business continuity. Using PowerShell, you can automate the backup process by creating scripts and scheduling them to run at regular intervals.

Example:
Automate a full system backup using PowerShell:

```powershell
$action = New-ScheduledTaskAction -Execute "PowerShell.exe" -Argument "-File C:\Scripts\Backup.ps1"
$trigger = New-ScheduledTaskTrigger -Daily -At "2:00AM"
Register-ScheduledTask -TaskName "DailyBackup" -Action $action -Trigger $trigger -Description "Automatic Daily Backup"
```

This example sets up a daily backup task at 2:00 AM, ensuring that your systems are backed up without manual intervention.

2. Automating Disk Cleanup:

Running disk cleanup regularly helps free up space on your drives, ensuring that your system performs optimally. PowerShell can automate the `Cleanmgr` utility or directly delete unnecessary files like temporary files or old log files.

Example:
Schedule a disk cleanup to run weekly:

```powershell
$action = New-ScheduledTaskAction -Execute "Cleanmgr.exe" -Argument "/sagerun:1"
$trigger = New-ScheduledTaskTrigger -Weekly -DaysOfWeek Monday -At "3:00AM"
Register-ScheduledTask -TaskName "DiskCleanup" -Action $action -Trigger $trigger -Description "Weekly Disk Cleanup"
```

3. Automating Software Updates:

Keeping software up to date is crucial for security and performance. Use PowerShell to automate the update process for applications, system patches, or even driver updates.

Example:
Schedule an automated task to update installed software using PowerShell and Windows Update:

```powershell
$action = New-ScheduledTaskAction -Execute "Powershell.exe" -Argument "Get-WindowsUpdate -AcceptAll -AutoReboot"
$trigger = New-ScheduledTaskTrigger -Monthly -At "4:00AM"
Register-ScheduledTask -TaskName "SoftwareUpdates" -Action $action -Trigger $trigger -Description "Monthly Software Updates"
```

4. Monitoring System Health:

Automating system health checks is a great way to ensure your infrastructure remains in top condition. You can write PowerShell scripts to check disk space, CPU usage, memory status, and more, and schedule them to run at regular intervals.

Example:

Schedule a task to monitor disk space and alert if the space is low:

```powershell
$action = New-ScheduledTaskAction -Execute "PowerShell.exe" -Argument "-File C:\Scripts\CheckDiskSpace.ps1"
$trigger = New-ScheduledTaskTrigger -Daily -At "6:00AM"
Register-ScheduledTask -TaskName "DiskSpaceMonitor" -Action $action -Trigger $trigger -Description "Daily Disk Space Check"
```

Task scheduling and automation are fundamental to effective IT operations. PowerShell provides the flexibility to schedule tasks easily and automate maintenance processes that would otherwise be time-consuming or prone to human error. By integrating PowerShell with Task Scheduler, IT professionals can ensure that critical tasks such as backups, software updates, system monitoring, and cleanup run reliably without manual intervention.

With a deeper understanding of PowerShell's task scheduling capabilities, you can automate your IT environment to improve efficiency, maintain system health, and reduce the burden of routine administrative tasks. Whether you're running routine maintenance scripts, automating system checks, or handling large-scale deployments, mastering task automation with PowerShell is a vital skill for today's IT professionals.

Automating IT tasks with PowerShell is a game-changer for IT professionals looking to streamline operations and increase productivity. By understanding how to leverage PowerShell's powerful cmdlets, functions, and scripts, you can take on repetitive and time-consuming tasks with ease. This chapter has provided a solid foundation in automating everyday IT functions, from user management to system configurations, enabling you to save both time and resources. As you continue to explore PowerShell's full potential, remember that automation is not just about speed—it's about creating more reliable, consistent, and error-free processes that contribute to the overall health of your IT environment. In the following chapters, we will continue to build on this foundation, introducing more advanced automation techniques that can take your scripts to the next level.

Chapter 4

Troubleshooting Servers Using PowerShell

In the fast-paced world of IT, server issues can arise at any moment, and when they do, time is of the essence. Troubleshooting efficiently can make the difference between resolving a problem quickly or letting it disrupt your operations. In this chapter, we will explore how PowerShell can become your best ally when it comes to diagnosing and fixing server-related problems. With its robust command-line tools and scripting capabilities, PowerShell empowers system administrators to quickly gather data, analyze system states, and implement solutions with precision.

From checking system logs to diagnosing network issues or monitoring performance, PowerShell offers a unified platform to streamline your troubleshooting efforts. Whether you are dealing with server crashes, slow performance, or misconfigured settings, this chapter will show you how to leverage PowerShell to quickly get to the root cause, saving both time and resources.

Network Troubleshooting

Network-related issues can often be elusive, and diagnosing them requires a systematic approach to identify connectivity problems, resolve configuration issues, and ensure proper communication between systems. PowerShell offers powerful cmdlets and techniques to aid in network troubleshooting, allowing IT professionals to test connectivity, investigate network configurations, and more.

Testing Network Connectivity with `Test-Connection` and `Test-NetConnection`

PowerShell provides the `Test-Connection` cmdlet, which is essentially a built-in version of the popular `ping` command, but with more flexibility and the ability to provide detailed output. It's an excellent starting point for diagnosing simple connectivity issues.

`Test-Connection`:
This cmdlet is used to send ICMP echo requests (pings) to a remote host to check for network connectivity. By default, `Test-Connection` pings a target four times, but you can customize the number of attempts or other parameters.

Example:

```powershell
Test-Connection -ComputerName www.example.com
```

This checks the network connectivity to `www.example.com`. If successful, the output will show round-trip times (RTT) for each ping attempt.

`Test-NetConnection`:
`Test-NetConnection` offers more advanced network diagnostics, such as checking the availability of specific ports, resolving DNS names, and performing TCP and ICMP tests.

Example:

```powershell
Test-NetConnection -ComputerName www.example.com -Port 80
```

This tests the network connection to `www.example.com` on port 80, which is used for HTTP traffic. You can specify different ports to check whether specific services are accessible.

`Test-NetConnection` is useful for determining the health of a network connection at a more granular level. It can provide details such as whether the remote host is reachable, whether a specific port is open, and any issues with the path between the local and remote machines.

Working with Network Adapters and IP Configurations

Another crucial aspect of network troubleshooting is understanding and managing the IP configuration of network adapters. In PowerShell, cmdlets like `Get-NetAdapter`, `Get-NetIPAddress`, and

`Set-NetIPAddress` give you the ability to query and modify network adapter settings.

Viewing Network Adapters:

You can use `Get-NetAdapter` to list all network interfaces (both physical and virtual) on a system and check their operational status, link speed, and other important details.

Example:

```powershell
Get-NetAdapter
```

This returns a list of all network adapters on the system, including their names, interface statuses (up/down), and more.

Checking IP Configuration:

To view the IP address configuration of all network adapters on the system, use the `Get-NetIPAddress` cmdlet. This provides detailed information on the IP addresses, subnet masks, and default gateways assigned to each network interface.

Example:

```powershell
Get-NetIPAddress
```

The output will show the IP addresses for each adapter, which can help you verify whether the network interface is configured properly.

Changing IP Configuration:
If you need to update or troubleshoot IP configurations, you can use `Set-NetIPAddress`. This cmdlet allows you to change the IP address, subnet mask, gateway, and other network settings.

Example:

```powershell
Set-NetIPAddress -InterfaceAlias "Ethernet" -IPAddress "192.168.1.100" -PrefixLength 24 -DefaultGateway "192.168.1.1"
```

This command configures the `Ethernet` interface with a new IP address, subnet mask (prefix length), and default gateway.

By understanding how to manipulate and troubleshoot network adapters and IP configurations using PowerShell, you can quickly identify network issues and make necessary adjustments.

Network troubleshooting is one of the most essential skills for IT professionals. With the right tools and strategies, you can identify connectivity problems and address them efficiently. PowerShell offers a comprehensive set of cmdlets to test network connectivity, check IP configurations, and manage network adapters—ensuring that you have everything you need to keep your systems running smoothly. Whether you are verifying connectivity with remote hosts, testing ports, or adjusting network settings, PowerShell simplifies the process and provides a unified approach to resolving network issues quickly and effectively.

Disk and Storage Troubleshooting

Disk and storage issues can be some of the most critical problems faced by IT administrators, often leading to slowdowns, data loss, or complete system failure if not addressed promptly. Identifying disk-related issues, monitoring space usage, and ensuring proper disk health are essential skills for every IT professional. PowerShell provides a robust set of cmdlets that can help you quickly diagnose disk problems, gather important information, and even automate storage management tasks. In this section, we will focus on querying disk information, identifying space issues, and generating useful reports to help troubleshoot and resolve disk and storage problems efficiently.

Querying Disk Information (`Get-Volume`, `Get-Disk`)

PowerShell provides several cmdlets to help you interact with disk and volume information. The most commonly used cmdlets for this purpose are `Get-Disk` and `Get-Volume`. Both cmdlets allow you to retrieve vital details about physical disks and logical volumes, which can help diagnose disk problems.

`Get-Disk`:
The `Get-Disk` cmdlet retrieves information about all the physical disks connected to the system, including their status, health, and partition styles. This cmdlet

provides an overview of the disk's health, including whether it's online, offline, or in a failed state.

Example:

```powershell
Get-Disk
```

This will return details about each disk on the system, including:
- Disk Number: Identifies the disk.
- Operational Status: Indicates whether the disk is online, offline, or in a warning/failure state.
- Health Status: Shows the health of the disk (e.g., Healthy, Unhealthy).
- Partition Style: Whether the disk uses MBR or GPT (GUID Partition Table).
- Size: The total size of the disk.

Example Output:

```plaintext
Number  FriendlyName  OperationalStatus  HealthStatus  Size
------  ------------  -----------------  ------------  ----
0       Samsung SSD   Online             Healthy       500 GB
1       Seagate HDD   Offline            Unhealthy     1 TB
```

This cmdlet can help identify whether a disk is healthy or has potential issues (such as being offline or failing).

`Get-Volume`:

The `Get-Volume` cmdlet provides information about the volumes on the disks, which are logical units used for storing data (e.g., C: drive, D: drive). This cmdlet can give you a deeper understanding of the space usage, file system type, and other volume-specific details.

Example:

```powershell
Get-Volume
```

This returns a list of all volumes, showing:
- Drive Letter: The drive letter assigned to the volume (e.g., C:, D:).
- File System: The file system in use (e.g., NTFS, ReFS).
- Size: The total size of the volume.
- Used Space: The amount of space currently in use.
- Free Space: The amount of available space.

Example Output:

```plaintext
    DriveLetter   FileSystem      Size    UsedSpace   FreeSpace
    -----------   -----------     -----   ---------   ---------
    C             NTFS            500 GB  300 GB      200 GB
    D             NTFS            1 TB    450 GB      550 GB
```

This cmdlet helps in quickly assessing how much free space is available on a volume, which is crucial when troubleshooting disk space issues.

Identifying Disk Space Issues and Generating Reports

Disk space problems can often go unnoticed until they cause critical system slowdowns or application failures. PowerShell's `Get-Volume` cmdlet, along with its ability to generate custom reports, can help you proactively monitor disk space usage.

Identifying Low Disk Space:

One of the most common disk-related issues is low disk space. By using `Get-Volume` and filtering for volumes with low available space, you can easily identify and address potential problems before they affect system performance.

Example:

```powershell
Get-Volume |
Where-Object {
$_.FreeSpace -lt 5GB }
```

This command will return a list of volumes with less than 5GB of free space, allowing you to take action (such as freeing up space, adding more storage, or alerting relevant personnel).

Generating Disk Space Reports:

PowerShell allows you to automate the generation of disk space reports, which can be useful for regular monitoring or for generating alerts. You can format the output in various ways, such as displaying it on-screen or exporting it to a file for later review.

Example (Export to CSV):

```powershell
Get-Volume | Select-Object DriveLetter, FileSystem, Size, UsedSpace, FreeSpace | Export-Csv -Path "C:\DiskSpaceReport.csv" -NoTypeInformation
```

This will export the disk space details for each volume to a CSV file, which can then be analyzed or sent to stakeholders.

Example (Display with Custom Formatting):

```powershell
Get-Volume | Format-Table -Property DriveLetter, FileSystem, @{Name="Used(GB)";Expression={[math]::round($_.UsedSpace/1GB, 2)}}, @{Name="Free(GB)";Expression={[math]::round($_.FreeSpace/1GB, 2)}}
```

This command will display the disk space in a user-friendly format, with the used and free space shown in gigabytes (GB).

Additional Tips for Disk and Storage Troubleshooting

Check Disk Health: Use the `Get-Disk` cmdlet to check for any potential disk failures or degraded health statuses. The cmdlet will show a "HealthStatus" column that can help identify disks that need immediate attention.

Example:

```powershell
Get-Disk | Where-Object {
$_.HealthStatus -ne 'Healthy'
}
```

This command will display any disks that are not in a healthy state, helping you identify failing disks before they cause issues.

Defragmentation and Optimization: PowerShell can also be used to trigger defragmentation or optimization of disks, especially on HDDs that suffer from fragmentation. While not directly part of troubleshooting, defragmenting can improve disk performance.

Example (Defragmenting a Disk):

```powershell
Optimize-Volume -DriveLetter C -Defrag
```

This will defragment the C: drive, potentially improving performance on mechanical hard drives.

Disk and storage problems can be some of the most pressing issues for IT administrators, but PowerShell provides a robust set of tools to troubleshoot and resolve them quickly. By utilizing cmdlets like `Get-Disk` and `Get-Volume`, you can identify hardware failures, assess disk space usage, and generate automated reports to stay on top of disk health. Armed with these techniques, you can ensure that disk-related issues are addressed promptly, preventing system slowdowns, data loss, or even catastrophic failures. PowerShell's capabilities for disk and storage troubleshooting make it an invaluable tool for maintaining optimal system performance and reliability.

Service and Application Monitoring

Effective service and application monitoring is crucial for ensuring the smooth operation of IT environments. Services that are not running properly or applications that are misbehaving can lead to system downtimes, user frustration, and lost productivity. PowerShell provides powerful cmdlets to help administrators monitor the health of services and applications in real-time, identify issues, and take corrective action when needed. In this section, we'll explore how to check the status of critical services, monitor application logs, and track performance counters to diagnose and resolve service-related issues efficiently.

Checking the Status of Critical Services

Windows services are essential components of the operating system that run in the background and perform various tasks like handling networking, managing print jobs, and running database systems. Monitoring the status of these services is vital for maintaining system stability and performance. PowerShell makes it simple to query the state of services, check whether they are running or stopped, and even take action if necessary.

`Get-Service`:

The `Get-Service` cmdlet allows you to retrieve information about the status of all services on a machine, or a specific service by name. The cmdlet shows whether the service is running, stopped, or in another state (e.g., paused, starting).

Example:

```powershell
Get-Service -Name "wuauserv"
```

This command checks the status of the Windows Update service (`wuauserv`). The output will show the service's status and other details such as its display name and the type of start-up (automatic, manual, etc.).

Example Output:

```plaintext
Status  Name        DisplayName
------  ----        -----------
Running wuauserv    Windows Update
```

If you need to check the status of all services, you can simply run:

```powershell
Get-Service
```

This will list all services, including their names, statuses, and start types.

Filtering Service Status:
You can also filter services by their status to quickly identify issues, such as stopped services or those that are experiencing problems.

Example (Get stopped services):

```powershell
Get-Service | Where-Object { $_.Status -eq 'Stopped' }
```

This will return a list of all services that are currently stopped, helping you identify those that may need to be started or investigated for failure.

Start, Stop, and Restart Services:
PowerShell also allows you to manage services directly from the command line. If a service is found to be stopped or malfunctioning, you can restart it or start it manually.

Example (Start a service):

```powershell
Start-Service -Name "wuauserv"
```

Example (Stop a service):

```powershell
Stop-Service -Name "wuauserv"
```

Example (Restart a service):

```powershell
Restart-Service -Name "wuauserv"
```

These commands can be useful for quickly resolving issues with services without needing to manually interact with the GUI or go through multiple steps.

Monitoring Application Logs and Performance Counters

Application logs and performance counters provide valuable insights into the health and performance of applications running on a system. By monitoring these logs, IT administrators can detect potential issues before they escalate, helping to ensure that applications are functioning properly and resources are being used efficiently.

Viewing Application Logs:

The Windows Event Log contains critical information about system, application, and security events. PowerShell allows you to easily query and filter these logs to find relevant information.

- `Get-EventLog`: This cmdlet retrieves event log entries from local or remote systems. You can use it to view application, system, or security logs, and filter by event types, IDs, and time ranges.

Example (Get application event logs):

```powershell
Get-EventLog -LogName Application -EntryType Error
```

This command retrieves error entries from the Application event log. You can change the `-EntryType` to "Information" or "Warning" depending on the level of severity you're interested in monitoring.

Example Output:

```plaintext
Source       TimeGenerated    Message
------       -------------    -------
Application  10/17/2024 5:30 PM  Application failed to start due to missing DLL
```

- Filtering Events: You can further filter logs based on time or event IDs. For example, to get the last 10 events from the Application log:

```powershell
Get-EventLog -LogName Application -Newest 10
```

This provides a quick snapshot of the most recent application-related issues that might need attention.

Using `Get-WinEvent`:
For more advanced querying and filtering, `Get-WinEvent` can be used. It provides more control over filtering by event log provider, and its output can be customized with detailed parameters.

Example (Get last 5 Application Errors):

```powershell
Get-WinEvent -LogName Application -MaxEvents 5 | Where-Object { $_.LevelDisplayName -eq "Error" }
```

This filters and shows the last 5 error-level events in the Application log.

Monitoring Performance Counters:
Performance counters are a powerful way to monitor the performance of applications and system resources, such as CPU usage, memory, disk IO, network throughput, and more. PowerShell provides cmdlets that allow you to access and query these counters in real-time.

`Get-Counter`:

The `Get-Counter` cmdlet retrieves performance counter data, such as the number of requests processed by a web server, CPU usage, or memory consumption. You can specify which counter to monitor by referencing its path.

Example (Monitor CPU Usage):

```powershell
Get-Counter '\Processor(_Total)\% Processor Time'
```

This retrieves the overall CPU usage as a percentage of time the processor is busy.

Example Output:

```plaintext
Timestamp                CounterSamples
---------                --------------
10/17/2024 10:30:00 AM   {69.35}
```

Monitoring Disk Usage:
To monitor disk activity, use the following command:

```powershell
Get-Counter '\LogicalDisk(_Total)\% Free Space'
```

This command will return the percentage of free space available on all logical disks.

By using performance counters, you can continuously monitor the performance of applications and servers, catching potential issues like resource exhaustion, memory leaks, or performance degradation before they impact users.

Service and application monitoring are vital for keeping systems running smoothly, and PowerShell offers the tools necessary to efficiently monitor services, track logs, and keep an eye on performance metrics. By leveraging cmdlets like `Get-Service`, `Get-EventLog`, and `Get-Counter`, IT administrators can quickly detect issues and take action to resolve them. Whether you're checking the status of critical services, filtering application logs for errors, or monitoring system performance in real-time, PowerShell's capabilities make it an indispensable tool for proactive service and application management. With these monitoring practices in place, you can ensure that your infrastructure remains stable, reliable, and performant.

Server Health and Performance

Maintaining server health and performance is crucial for ensuring that IT systems are operating efficiently and reliably. Regular monitoring and diagnostics can help identify issues before they escalate, minimize downtime, and optimize the overall performance of your infrastructure. PowerShell provides a robust set of tools to help you diagnose server issues, monitor system performance, and generate reports that provide insights into the health of your servers. In this section, we will explore how to use cmdlets like `Get-Process`, `Get-EventLog`, and performance counters to monitor system resources, as well as how to generate health reports that give administrators a comprehensive overview of server status.

Using `Get-Process` for System Diagnostics

The `Get-Process` cmdlet is one of the most essential tools for monitoring the performance of a system. It allows administrators to retrieve a list of all running processes, including detailed information on CPU usage, memory consumption, and other resource utilization.

Listing Running Processes:

The `Get-Process` cmdlet is used to get a list of processes that are currently running on a local or remote machine. This can help identify processes that are consuming excessive resources or may be causing performance degradation.

Example:

```powershell
Get-Process
```

This command returns a list of all processes currently running, along with key details such as process name, ID, CPU usage, and memory consumption.

Example Output:

```plaintext
NPM(K)    PM(K)    WS(K)   VM(M)   CPU(s)     Id  ProcessName
------    -----    -----   -----   ------     --  -----------
    45    10240    20480    3000    25.64   1234  chrome
    38     2048    10240    1024    10.12   5678  powershell
```

By reviewing the output of `Get-Process`, administrators can easily identify resource hogs and take corrective actions, such as terminating unnecessary processes or optimizing resource allocation.

Filtering and Sorting Process Data:

You can filter or sort the list of processes based on specific criteria. For example, to list only processes that are using more than 100MB of memory:

```powershell
Get-Process | Where-Object { $_.WorkingSet -gt 100MB }
```

To sort processes by CPU usage:

```powershell
Get-Process | Sort-Object CPU -Descending
```

This can help prioritize which processes to investigate further for optimization or troubleshooting.

Using `Get-EventLog` for System Diagnostics

Event logs are a critical source of diagnostic information about system health, errors, and performance issues. The `Get-EventLog` cmdlet allows administrators to query event logs for specific information related to system health and performance.

Retrieving System and Application Event Logs:

The `Get-EventLog` cmdlet allows you to retrieve logs related to system events, application errors, and security issues. By reviewing these logs, administrators can spot system warnings, errors, or failures that may indicate underlying issues affecting server performance.

Example (Get system event logs):

```powershell
Get-EventLog -LogName System -Newest 10
```

This retrieves the 10 most recent entries from the system event log. You can filter event types, specify time ranges, and search for specific event IDs related to performance issues, hardware failures, or system crashes.

Example Output:

```plaintext
Source              TimeGenerated       Message
------              --------------      -------
Microsoft-Windows-Disk   10/17/2024 4:15 PM   Disk space low on C: drive
Service Control Manager  10/17/2024 4:10 PM   Service 'wuauserv' stopped unexpectedly
```

Finding and Handling Specific Errors:

If you're troubleshooting a specific issue, such as disk space or a service failure, you can filter event logs based on the error type or event ID.

Example (Filter for disk-related issues):

```powershell
Get-EventLog -LogName System | Where-Object { $_.Message -like "*disk*low*" }
```

165

This command searches the system event logs for entries related to low disk space, making it easier to quickly identify and address disk performance issues.

Using Performance Counters for Server Diagnostics

Performance counters provide real-time data on system resource usage, allowing administrators to monitor key performance metrics like CPU load, memory consumption, disk I/O, and network activity. PowerShell provides access to these counters, enabling continuous monitoring and automated diagnostics.

Monitoring CPU Usage:
You can track CPU usage across the system using the `Get-Counter` cmdlet. This allows you to monitor how much processing power is being consumed by the CPU, which is essential for identifying performance bottlenecks.

Example:
```
```powershell
Get-Counter '\Processor(_Total)\% Processor Time'
```
```

This command retrieves the overall percentage of CPU usage across all cores in the system. High CPU usage over extended periods may indicate resource-intensive processes or applications that need attention.

Monitoring Memory Usage:

Memory usage is another critical aspect of server performance. The `Get-Counter` cmdlet can be used to monitor memory utilization, including available memory and committed memory.

Example:

```powershell
Get-Counter '\Memory\Available MBytes'
```

This command checks the available memory in MB. If the available memory is low, it could indicate that the system is under memory pressure and may need optimization or additional resources.

Monitoring Disk Usage:

Disk space and disk activity are crucial for server health. You can use performance counters to monitor disk usage and detect potential disk-related issues such as low disk space or high disk activity.

Example (Monitor disk space usage):

```powershell
Get-Counter '\LogicalDisk(_Total)\% Free Space'
```

This command monitors the percentage of free space on all logical disks. If free space is low, it could affect system performance, and action should be taken to free up space or add additional storage.

Monitoring Network Usage:
Network connectivity and bandwidth usage are vital for server performance, especially in a multi-server environment. PowerShell can retrieve performance counters for network adapters to track network traffic and identify any bottlenecks or failures.

Example:

```powershell
Get-Counter '\Network Interface(*)\Bytes Total/sec'
```

This monitors the total bytes being sent and received per second across all network interfaces on the server.

Generating Server Health Reports

Once you've gathered diagnostic data from processes, event logs, and performance counters, it's time to compile and analyze this information. PowerShell allows you to export the results of these commands to text files, CSV files, or even directly into the Event Log for future reference.

Exporting Data to CSV:

Exporting performance data to CSV format enables you to generate comprehensive health reports that can be analyzed later.

Example (Export system health data):

```powershell
Get-Process | Select-Object Name, CPU, Memory | Export-Csv "C:\server_health_report.csv" -NoTypeInformation
```

This command exports a CSV file containing the process name, CPU usage, and memory usage for each process on the system, providing an easy-to-read report of the current system state.

Automating Report Generation:

You can automate the process of generating server health reports by scheduling PowerShell scripts to run at regular intervals. This ensures that you continuously monitor server health without needing to manually intervene.

Example (Schedule a server health report):

```powershell
$scriptPath = "C:\scripts\server_health.ps1"
$trigger = New-ScheduledTaskTrigger -Daily -At "2:00AM"
Register-ScheduledTask -Action (New-ScheduledTaskAction -Execute "powershell.exe" -Argument $scriptPath) -Trigger $trigger -TaskName "ServerHealthReport"
```

This command sets up a scheduled task to generate a server health report every day at 2:00 AM.

Regularly monitoring server health and performance is essential for maintaining the reliability of IT systems. By using PowerShell cmdlets like `Get-Process`, `Get-EventLog`, and performance counters, administrators can proactively identify issues related to system resources, services, and applications. Furthermore, by automating server health reporting and diagnostics, you ensure that your infrastructure remains optimized and ready to handle the demands of the organization. With the tools and techniques outlined in this section, administrators can better manage and troubleshoot server health, improving uptime, reducing system failures, and increasing operational efficiency.

Automating Troubleshooting Tasks

In IT operations, troubleshooting is an essential task that ensures the smooth functioning of servers and services. However, manual troubleshooting can be time-consuming, especially when problems recur frequently. PowerShell allows IT professionals to automate common troubleshooting tasks, such as system checks, service restarts, and error reporting, making the process more efficient and proactive. Additionally, automating alerts for system failures or performance issues ensures that administrators are immediately notified of any potential problems before they escalate, minimizing downtime and preventing service interruptions.

This section will explore how to create PowerShell scripts to automate troubleshooting actions and set up alerts to notify administrators of critical issues.

Creating Scripts to Automate Common Troubleshooting Actions

Automating common troubleshooting tasks with PowerShell scripts can significantly reduce the time spent on reactive maintenance and improve system uptime. A simple PowerShell script can be created to address recurring issues such as restarting failed services, clearing log files, or checking for disk space.

Restarting Failed Services Automatically:
One common troubleshooting action is restarting a service that has stopped unexpectedly. A PowerShell script can be written to check the status of services and restart them if they are found to be stopped or unresponsive.

Example (Restart a service if it stops):

```powershell
$serviceName = "wuauserv"  # Windows Update Service

$serviceStatus = Get-Service -Name $serviceName

if ($serviceStatus.Status -eq 'Stopped') {
    Write-Host "$serviceName is stopped. Restarting..."
    Start-Service -Name $serviceName
    Write-Host "$serviceName has been restarted."
}
else {
    Write-Host "$serviceName is running."
}
```

In this example, the script checks whether the "Windows Update" service (`wuauserv`) is stopped. If the service is stopped, the script restarts it. Automating this task ensures that critical services are kept running without the need for manual intervention.

Clearing Event Logs After Troubleshooting:

Event logs can become cluttered with diagnostic messages, errors, and warnings after troubleshooting. You can automate the process of clearing event logs once the troubleshooting process is complete.

Example (Clear application event log):

```powershell
Clear-EventLog -LogName Application
Write-Host "Application event log cleared."
```

This script clears the "Application" log after troubleshooting, ensuring that old log entries are removed, making it easier to spot new errors and issues.

Checking Disk Space and Sending an Alert:
Disk space issues can cause significant disruptions, so it's important to regularly check available disk space and address low storage issues. You can automate a check for disk space, and if it falls below a certain threshold, send an email alert or log the issue for follow-up.

Example (Check disk space and alert if low):

```powershell
$diskSpace = Get-PSDrive C

if ($diskSpace.Used -gt $diskSpace.Maximum - 10GB) {
    Write-Host "Warning: Disk space on C: is running low!"
    Send-MailMessage -From "admin@domain.com" -To "support@domain.com" -Subject "Disk Space Warning" -Body "Disk space on C: drive is low. Immediate action is needed." -SmtpServer "smtp.domain.com"
}
else {
   Write-Host "Disk space on C: is sufficient."
}
```

In this example, the script checks the disk space on the C: drive. If the used space exceeds the maximum available space by more than 10 GB, it sends an email notification to the system administrator.

Setting Up Alerts for System Failures or Performance Issues

Setting up alerts to automatically notify administrators of system failures or performance issues is a proactive approach to IT management. With PowerShell, you can monitor a wide range of performance metrics (such as

CPU usage, memory usage, and disk space) and set up email alerts or system notifications when certain thresholds are exceeded.

Setting Up Performance Alerts:

You can create a script that monitors specific performance counters (such as CPU usage or memory consumption) and sends an alert if they exceed predefined thresholds.

Example (Monitor CPU usage and send an alert if high):

```powershell
$cpuUsage = Get-Counter '\Processor(_Total)\% Processor Time'

if ($cpuUsage.CounterSamples[0].CookedValue -gt 90) {
   Write-Host "Warning: CPU usage is over 90%."
   Send-MailMessage -From "admin@domain.com" -To "support@domain.com" -Subject "CPU Usage Alert" -Body "CPU usage is over 90%. Please investigate." -SmtpServer "smtp.domain.com"
}
else {
   Write-Host "CPU usage is normal."
}
```

This script checks the overall CPU usage and sends an email alert if the CPU usage exceeds 90%. This ensures that system administrators are informed of performance issues before they lead to system slowdowns or failures.

Setting Up Disk Space Alerts:

As with the disk space check example earlier, you can create a script that continuously monitors disk space and sends an alert when the free space is running low.

Example (Monitor disk space and alert if less than 10 GB free):

```powershell
$diskSpace = Get-PSDrive C

if ($diskSpace.Free -lt 10GB) {
    Write-Host "Warning: Less than 10GB of free space on C: drive."
      Send-MailMessage -From "admin@domain.com" -To "support@domain.com" -Subject "Disk Space Alert" -Body "Free space on C: drive is low. Please take action." -SmtpServer "smtp.domain.com"
}
else {
   Write-Host "Disk space is adequate."
}
```

This script monitors free space on the C: drive, sending an alert if the free space drops below 10 GB.

Scheduling and Automating Troubleshooting Tasks

PowerShell allows you to automate the execution of troubleshooting tasks using the Windows Task Scheduler. By scheduling scripts to run at specific intervals or when certain events occur, you ensure that common troubleshooting actions are handled automatically.

Scheduling a Script to Run Automatically:
PowerShell scripts can be scheduled to run periodically, ensuring that troubleshooting tasks like service checks, disk space monitoring, and performance alerts are executed regularly.

Example (Schedule a script to run daily):

```powershell
$scriptPath = "C:\scripts\disk_space_check.ps1"
$trigger = New-ScheduledTaskTrigger -Daily -At "3:00AM"
Register-ScheduledTask -Action (New-ScheduledTaskAction -Execute "powershell.exe" -Argument $scriptPath) -Trigger $trigger -TaskName "DailyDiskSpaceCheck"
```

This script sets up a scheduled task that runs a disk space check script every day at 3:00 AM. The task will automatically run the script, which checks the disk space and sends alerts if necessary.

Automating troubleshooting tasks with PowerShell not only saves time and resources but also ensures a proactive approach to system health. By creating scripts to automatically check services, disk space, CPU usage, and other key system metrics, administrators can catch potential problems before they affect end users. Setting up automated alerts further enhances this by notifying administrators in real time about critical issues, allowing them to take swift action and prevent system failures. PowerShell's ability to automate these routine tasks is a powerful tool that ensures your systems remain reliable, optimized, and well-maintained without requiring constant manual intervention.

Effective server troubleshooting is a key skill for any IT professional, and PowerShell provides the tools to make this process more efficient and reliable. With its deep integration into Windows Server environments, PowerShell allows you to gather detailed information, pinpoint issues, and apply fixes swiftly. By mastering the PowerShell cmdlets and strategies discussed in this chapter, you will be better equipped to handle the inevitable server challenges that arise, ensuring minimal downtime and maximum productivity. By using PowerShell as your troubleshooting toolkit, you'll be able to diagnose problems more effectively, automate solutions, and maintain smooth server operations with ease.

Chapter 5

Managing Users and Active Directory with PowerShell

Managing users and their permissions is a core responsibility for IT administrators, particularly in environments using Active Directory (AD). Whether you're adding new users, modifying their roles, or handling group memberships, PowerShell is an indispensable tool that simplifies these tasks. With its powerful scripting capabilities, PowerShell enables you to automate user management processes, reduce manual errors, and streamline your workflow.

In this chapter, we'll explore how to leverage PowerShell to efficiently manage users, groups, and organizational units (OUs) in Active Directory. From creating and modifying user accounts to managing permissions and group memberships, you'll learn how to handle these critical tasks with precision and ease. With PowerShell's flexibility, you'll not only automate administrative tasks but also ensure a more secure and efficient management of your organization's IT infrastructure.

Creating and Managing User Accounts

Managing user accounts is one of the most common tasks for administrators, and PowerShell provides a streamlined approach to handle this efficiently. Whether you're creating new users, modifying their details, or deleting outdated accounts, PowerShell offers several cmdlets designed specifically for these operations. This section will guide you through the process of managing user accounts in Active Directory using key cmdlets like `New-ADUser`, `Set-ADUser`, and `Remove-ADUser`. Additionally, we'll cover how to automate bulk user creation from CSV files, a critical task for environments where employees are regularly onboarded or offboarded.

Creating New User Accounts

The cmdlet `New-ADUser` is used to create a new user in Active Directory. It allows you to specify various attributes such as the user's name, username, password, and which Organizational Unit (OU) the user should belong to.

```powershell
New-ADUser -SamAccountName "jdoe" -Name "John Doe" -GivenName "John" -Surname "Doe" -DisplayName "John Doe" -UserPrincipalName "jdoe@company.com" -Path "OU=Employees,DC=company,DC=com" -AccountPassword (ConvertTo-SecureString "TempP@ssword" -AsPlainText -Force) -Enabled $true
```

This command creates a new user named "John Doe" with the username "jdoe" and a temporary password "TempP@ssword". You can also specify the Organizational Unit where the user account will be placed, which is useful in larger environments where you may have different OUs for various departments.

Modifying User Accounts

Once a user account is created, you might need to modify various properties, such as updating the user's title, department, or email address. The `Set-ADUser` cmdlet allows you to change these attributes. Here's how you can modify a user's department and phone number:

```powershell
Set-ADUser -Identity "jdoe" -Title "Senior Developer" -Department "Engineering" -OfficePhone "555-1234"
```

This command updates John Doe's department and office phone number in Active Directory. You can update several attributes at once or individually, depending on your needs.

Deleting User Accounts

Removing a user who is no longer part of the organization is just as straightforward. The `Remove-ADUser` cmdlet is used to delete user accounts from Active Directory. To remove the user "John Doe", for example:

```powershell
Remove-ADUser
-Identity "jdoe"
```

This will permanently delete the user from Active Directory. You can also add the `-WhatIf` parameter to test the removal without actually deleting the account, which is a good practice when running any destructive command.

Bulk User Creation from CSV Files

In larger organizations, it's common to onboard multiple employees at once. Instead of manually creating each user, you can automate this process by importing user data from a CSV file. PowerShell allows you to bulk-create users by reading a CSV file and iterating over its contents. Here's how it works:

1. Prepare the CSV file: Your CSV file should contain the necessary user data, such as first name, last name, department, and username. For example:

```csv
FirstName,LastName,Username,Department,Email
John,Doe,jdoe,Engineering,jdoe@company.com
Jane,Smith,jsmith,Marketing,jsmith@company.com
```

2. **Script to Import and Create Users:**

```powershell
$users = Import-Csv "C:\path\to\users.csv"
foreach ($user in $users) {
    New-ADUser -SamAccountName $user.Username -Name "$($user.FirstName) $($user.LastName)" -GivenName $user.FirstName -Surname $user.LastName -DisplayName "$($user.FirstName) $($user.LastName)" -UserPrincipalName $user.Email -Department $user.Department -Path "OU=Employees,DC=company,DC=com" -AccountPassword (ConvertTo-SecureString "TempP@ssword" -AsPlainText -Force) -Enabled $true
}
```

This script will read the data from the CSV file and create user accounts for each line in the file. The attributes are dynamically pulled from the CSV, making bulk user creation a simple task.

Managing user accounts with PowerShell can save time, reduce errors, and improve consistency, particularly in larger environments where manual user creation becomes tedious. With the `New-ADUser`, `Set-ADUser`, and `Remove-ADUser` cmdlets, you have powerful tools at your disposal to handle user accounts efficiently. Furthermore, automating bulk user creation from CSV files is an essential technique that IT professionals can use to speed up user provisioning and ensure accuracy. By mastering these skills, you will be better equipped to manage a dynamic and secure Active Directory environment.

Managing Active Directory Groups

Active Directory (AD) groups are an essential component for managing permissions, organizing users, and applying security policies within an enterprise environment. Groups allow you to assign common permissions to multiple users, which simplifies administration and ensures consistent access control across the network. PowerShell provides powerful cmdlets to add, remove, and manage users within AD groups, as well as to configure the group membership and their associated permissions.

Adding Users to Active Directory Groups

Adding users to groups is one of the most frequent administrative tasks in any organization. With PowerShell, you can add users to one or more groups efficiently. The cmdlet used to add a user to an AD group is `Add-ADGroupMember`.

Here's an example of how to add a user to a specific group:

```powershell
Add-ADGroupMember -Identity "Engineering" -Members "jdoe"
```

In this example, the user "jdoe" is added to the "Engineering" group. You can specify the group using the `-Identity` parameter and the user with the `-Members` parameter. This command can be used for adding a single user, or you can add multiple users by separating their names with commas:

```powershell
Add-ADGroupMember -Identity "Engineering" -Members "jdoe", "jsmith", "mbrown"
```

If you're working with a large number of users, you can import the users from a CSV file, much like we did with user creation:

```powershell
$users = Import-Csv "C:\path\to\users.csv"
foreach ($user in $users) {
    Add-ADGroupMember -Identity $user.Group -Members $user.Username
}
```

This method reads the CSV file, where each user's group and username are listed, and adds each user to the appropriate group.

Removing Users from Active Directory Groups

Just as easily as you can add users, you can also remove them from groups using the `Remove-ADGroupMember` cmdlet. Removing users from groups is necessary when an employee changes departments or leaves the organization, as you need to revoke their access to certain resources associated with the group.

Here's an example:

```powershell
Remove-ADGroupMember -Identity "Engineering" -Members "jdoe" -Confirm:$false
```

The `-Confirm:$false` parameter bypasses the confirmation prompt, making the command more suitable for scripting. To remove multiple users, separate their usernames with commas:

```powershell
Remove-ADGroupMember -Identity "Engineering" -Members "jdoe", "jsmith", "mbrown" -Confirm:$false
```

Again, bulk operations are also possible with CSV imports, just as with adding users:

```powershell
$users = Import-Csv "C:\path\to\users.csv"
foreach ($user in $users) {
    Remove-ADGroupMember -Identity $user.Group -Members $user.Username -Confirm:$false
}
```

Managing Group Membership and Permissions

Managing group membership and permissions in Active Directory is crucial for ensuring the right users have the appropriate access to resources. Beyond adding and removing users from groups, you need to understand how groups are used in conjunction with permissions.

Viewing Group Membership

PowerShell allows you to list all members of a group using the `Get-ADGroupMember` cmdlet. This is useful for auditing purposes and when you need to review who has access to a specific resource:

```powershell
Get-ADGroupMember -Identity "Engineering"
```

This command will list all users and nested groups that are members of the "Engineering" group. You can also use the `-Recursive` parameter to include members of nested groups.

```powershell
Get-ADGroupMember
-Identity "Engineering"
-Recursive
```

Changing Group Types

In Active Directory, groups can be either Security Groups or Distribution Groups. Security Groups are used for assigning permissions, while Distribution Groups are used for email distribution lists. You can check the type of a group and change it as needed:

To check the type of group:

```powershell
Get-ADGroup -Identity "Engineering" | Select-Object Name, GroupCategory
```

If you need to convert a distribution group to a security group, use the following command:

```powershell
Set-ADGroup -Identity "Engineering" -GroupCategory Security
```

You can also change the scope of the group (whether it's *Global*, *Domain Local*, or *Universal*), depending on your needs for resource access across domains or forests:

```powershell
Set-ADGroup -Identity "Engineering" -GroupScope Global
```

Assigning Permissions to Groups

After managing group membership, it's important to understand how permissions are assigned to groups. Permissions can be granted on file systems, SharePoint, Exchange, and other resources, and assigning a group to these resources allows all members of that group to inherit the associated permissions.

To assign permissions to a folder or file for a specific group, you can use `Set-Acl` along with `Get-Acl` to modify Access Control Lists (ACLs). For example:

```powershell
$acl = Get-Acl "C:\SharedFolder"
$permission = "Domain\Engineering", "Modify"
$accessRule = New-Object System.Security.AccessControl.FileSystemAccessRule($permission, "Modify", "Allow")
$acl.AddAccessRule($accessRule)
Set-Acl "C:\SharedFolder" $acl
```

This script adds a "Modify" permission for the "Engineering" group to the folder `C:\SharedFolder`.

Managing Active Directory groups is a crucial part of ensuring that users have the right level of access to network resources. PowerShell simplifies the process of adding and removing users from groups, whether individually or in bulk, and helps ensure consistency and efficiency in group management. Additionally, understanding how to modify group properties, view group memberships, and assign permissions enables administrators to tailor access controls to meet the needs of the organization. By mastering these tasks, administrators can better manage their organization's security and access policies, streamlining operations and reducing the risk of unauthorized access.

Automating Active Directory Tasks

Active Directory (AD) administration can quickly become time-consuming, especially in large environments with numerous users and groups. Automating common AD tasks not only reduces the manual effort but also minimizes the risk of errors, ensuring consistency and reliability across your organization. PowerShell provides robust cmdlets and scripting capabilities that allow administrators to automate routine AD tasks such as password resets, group membership modifications, and reporting on user and group status.

In this section, we'll cover how to automate some of the most common AD administrative tasks, such as resetting passwords, managing group memberships, and generating reports, as well as creating scripts for AD health checks.

Automating Password Resets

One of the most common tasks for Active Directory administrators is resetting user passwords. This is often requested by users who forget their passwords, or as part of regular security protocols. Automating password resets with PowerShell can save time and ensure that the process is done consistently.

To reset a user's password in Active Directory, you can use the `Set-ADAccountPassword` cmdlet. Here's an example of resetting a single user's password:

```powershell
Set-ADAccountPassword -Identity "jdoe" -NewPassword (ConvertTo-SecureString -String "NewPassword123!" -AsPlainText -Force) -Reset
```

This command resets the password of user "jdoe" to "NewPassword123!". Note that the `ConvertTo-SecureString` cmdlet is used to convert the plain-text password to a secure string.

To automate password resets for multiple users, you can import a list of usernames (e.g., from a CSV file) and iterate through each entry to reset their passwords:

```powershell
$users = Import-Csv "C:\path\to\users.csv"
foreach ($user in $users) {
    Set-ADAccountPassword -Identity $user.Username -NewPassword (ConvertTo-SecureString -String $user.NewPassword -AsPlainText -Force) -Reset
}
```

In this example, the CSV file contains the usernames and new passwords for each user. The script reads each entry and resets their password automatically.

Automating Group Membership Changes

Managing group memberships is another task that can benefit from automation, especially when users frequently change departments or roles. Adding or removing users from groups can be done with

PowerShell's `Add-ADGroupMember` and `Remove-ADGroupMember` cmdlets.

To automate adding or removing users based on a specific condition (e.g., changing departments), you can write a script that reads a CSV file of users and their desired group memberships. For example, to bulk add users to a group:

```powershell
$users = Import-Csv "C:\path\to\users.csv"
foreach ($user in $users) {
    Add-ADGroupMember -Identity $user.Group -Members $user.Username
}
```

In this script, the CSV file contains the usernames and their corresponding group names. The script reads the file and adds the users to their assigned groups.

To remove users from a group, you can use a similar approach:

```powershell
$users = Import-Csv "C:\path\to\users.csv"
foreach ($user in $users) {
    Remove-ADGroupMember -Identity $user.Group -Members $user.Username -Confirm:$false
}
```

This will remove each user from the specified group automatically.

Scripting User Reports

Generating reports on Active Directory users is an important part of regular AD administration. These reports can provide insights into user properties, group memberships, and account status. PowerShell makes it easy to create detailed user reports, which can be used for audits, compliance, and troubleshooting.

A simple script to generate a report of all users in Active Directory, including their names, usernames, and account status, could look like this:

```powershell
Get-ADUser -Filter * -Property Name, SamAccountName, Enabled | Select-Object Name, SamAccountName, Enabled | Export-Csv "C:\path\to\user_report.csv" -NoTypeInformation
```

This script retrieves all users in the AD and selects their `Name`, `SamAccountName`, and `Enabled` status. It then exports the results to a CSV file for further analysis.

To create more detailed reports, you can include additional properties, such as department, last login time, or expiration date:

```powershell
Get-ADUser -Filter * -Property Name, SamAccountName, Department, LastLogonDate, AccountExpirationDate | Select-Object Name, SamAccountName, Department, LastLogonDate, AccountExpirationDate | Export-Csv "C:\path\to\detailed_user_report.csv" -NoTypeInformation
```

This enhanced report includes the department, last logon time, and account expiration date for each user, making it ideal for a more comprehensive audit.

Active Directory Health Checks

Performing regular health checks on Active Directory is crucial to ensure that it is functioning properly. Automated health checks can help identify issues before they affect users or services. Some common health check tasks include checking for replication issues, monitoring domain controller health, and verifying the status of key services.

A simple script to check the health of domain controllers and identify replication issues might look like this:

```powershell
Get-ADReplicationPartnerMetadata -Scope Domain | Select-Object Server, LastSyncResult, LastSyncTime
```

This script checks the status of domain controller replication, listing the server, the result of the last replication attempt, and the time of the last successful sync.

To monitor the health of Active Directory services, you can use the `Get-Service` cmdlet to check if key AD services (such as the Kerberos Key Distribution Center or Active Directory Domain Services) are running:

```powershell
Get-Service -Name "kdc", "ntds" | Select-Object Name, Status
```

This will return the status of the Kerberos and AD Domain Services, letting you know if they are running or stopped.

Automating Active Directory tasks with PowerShell is one of the most efficient ways to save time, reduce human error, and ensure consistency across your network. From resetting passwords and managing group memberships to generating reports and performing health checks, PowerShell makes these tasks not only possible but highly efficient. By implementing automation scripts, IT administrators can streamline their workload, ensure accurate administration, and proactively address issues, keeping Active Directory environments secure and running smoothly.

Querying AD Data

Querying Active Directory (AD) data is a fundamental task for administrators, allowing them to retrieve valuable information about users, groups, organizational units (OUs), and other directory objects. PowerShell provides powerful cmdlets to interact with and extract AD data, making it possible to query and manipulate user, group, and OU information efficiently.

In this section, we'll explore how to retrieve AD data using the `Get-ADUser`, `Get-ADGroup`, and other cmdlets, as well as how to filter, format, and export the results into useful reports.

Retrieving User Data with `Get-ADUser`

The `Get-ADUser` cmdlet is used to retrieve information about users in Active Directory. You can query specific users or retrieve data for all users in the domain.

To retrieve a specific user's details, you can use the following command:

```powershell
Get-ADUser -Identity "jdoe" -Properties *
```

This command fetches all properties of the user "jdoe". The `-Properties` flag ensures that all available properties for the user are returned, including attributes like email address, department, and group memberships.

If you need to retrieve a list of all users in the domain, you can run:

```powershell
Get-ADUser -Filter * -Properties Name, SamAccountName, Department
```

This command retrieves the names, SamAccountNames (usernames), and department information for all users in the domain.

Retrieving Group Data with `Get-ADGroup`

The `Get-ADGroup` cmdlet is used to retrieve information about AD groups. This can include groups to which users belong, or the attributes of the groups themselves, such as group membership type and scope.

For instance, to retrieve information about a specific group, use the following command:

```powershell
Get-ADGroup -Identity "SalesTeam" -Properties *
```

This command will return all properties of the "SalesTeam" group.

To retrieve all groups in your domain, simply run:

```powershell
Get-ADGroup -Filter *
-Properties Name,
GroupCategory,
GroupScope
```

This will display the names of all groups, along with their category (e.g., Security or Distribution) and scope (e.g., Global, Domain Local).

Retrieving Organizational Unit (OU) Data with `Get-ADOrganizationalUnit`

The `Get-ADOrganizationalUnit` cmdlet allows administrators to query OUs within the domain. You can use this cmdlet to list OUs or retrieve specific information about a given OU.

To list all OUs in the domain, you can run:

```powershell
Get-ADOrganizationalUnit -Filter * -Properties Name, DistinguishedName
```

This command will display the names and distinguished names (DNs) of all OUs.

To retrieve the properties of a specific OU, use:

```powershell
Get-ADOrganizationalUnit -Identity "Sales" -Properties *
```

This command returns detailed properties for the "Sales" OU, including its distinguished name, managedBy attribute, and description.

Filtering AD Data

Filtering is essential when you're working with large directories or need specific data from the results. You can filter the data based on specific attributes such as group membership, user status, or department.

For example, to retrieve all users who are part of the "HR" department, you can filter the `Get-ADUser` results like this:

```powershell
Get-ADUser -Filter {Department -eq "HR"} -Properties Name, SamAccountName, Department
```

This will return all users whose department is "HR". Similarly, you can filter users who are enabled:

```powershell
Get-ADUser -Filter {Enabled -eq $true} -Properties Name, SamAccountName, Enabled
```

This query retrieves only the enabled users in Active Directory.

Exporting Results to CSV or HTML Reports

Once you've queried the data, you may want to export it for reporting, analysis, or record-keeping. PowerShell allows you to easily export AD data to various formats, including CSV and HTML, using the `Export-Csv` and `ConvertTo-Html` cmdlets.

To export the list of users in a specific department to a CSV file, use:

```powershell
Get-ADUser -Filter {Department -eq "HR"} -Properties Name, SamAccountName, Department | Export-Csv "C:\path\to\hr_users.csv" -NoTypeInformation
```

This command retrieves all users in the "HR" department and exports the results to a CSV file, without including type information.

You can also generate an HTML report of your query results:

```powershell
Get-ADGroup -Filter * -Properties Name, GroupCategory, GroupScope | ConvertTo-Html -Property Name, GroupCategory, GroupScope | Out-File "C:\path\to\groups_report.html"
```

This will generate an HTML report of all groups, including their name, category, and scope, and save it to a file.

Advanced Filtering and Queries

PowerShell also supports advanced filtering, such as querying for users based on multiple attributes. For instance, you can query users who belong to a specific department *and* have been inactive for more than 30 days:

```powershell
Get-ADUser -Filter {Department -eq "HR" -and LastLogonDate -lt (Get-Date).AddDays(-30)} -Properties Name, LastLogonDate | Export-Csv "C:\path\to\inactive_hr_users.csv" -NoTypeInformation
```

This command retrieves users from the "HR" department who have not logged in for more than 30 days and exports the results to a CSV file.

Querying Active Directory data with PowerShell provides administrators with a fast, flexible way to extract and analyze information from the directory. Whether you need to retrieve user, group, or OU data, PowerShell's cmdlets allow you to filter and format the results in a way that meets your needs. By exporting data to CSV or HTML, you can generate reports for auditing, compliance, or troubleshooting purposes. Mastering these querying techniques is an essential skill for any IT professional, allowing you to manage and monitor your AD environment efficiently and effectively.

Mastering Active Directory management with PowerShell is a game-changer for IT professionals. By automating common user management tasks—such as creating user accounts, managing group memberships, and modifying permissions—you can save time, reduce human error, and ensure consistent and secure administration. Whether you're working with on-premises AD or Azure AD, PowerShell provides the tools necessary for efficient user and group management. In this chapter, you've gained a deeper understanding of how to simplify and automate Active Directory tasks, empowering you to optimize your IT operations with minimal manual intervention.

Chapter 6

Reporting and Auditing with PowerShell

Reporting and auditing are vital tasks for IT professionals, ensuring that system activities are tracked, compliance requirements are met, and security is maintained. PowerShell makes reporting and auditing simple yet powerful by enabling you to gather detailed system data, analyze logs, and generate custom reports with ease. In this chapter, we'll explore how to use PowerShell to create meaningful reports and perform audits on various aspects of your IT infrastructure, such as user activity, system performance, and security settings. Whether you're managing a small network or an enterprise environment, mastering these techniques will enhance your ability to keep systems running smoothly and meet organizational standards.

Generating System Reports:

Creating Custom Reports for Servers, Users, and Network Devices

PowerShell's flexibility allows you to create highly customizable reports for a variety of system resources, including servers, users, and network devices. To generate these reports, you can query system information using specific cmdlets that provide data on servers, Active Directory users, and network devices. The `Get-Command`, `Get-Process`, `Get-EventLog`, `Get-ADUser`, `Get-NetAdapter`, and other cmdlets can be used to collect relevant data that needs to be included in your reports.

1. Servers: To generate a report of server status or performance, you can use cmdlets such as `Get-Process` for running processes, `Get-EventLog` for event logs, and `Get-Volume` for storage information. These can be filtered and formatted to suit the needs of your report.

Example: To generate a report for server performance, you could use:

```powershell
Get-Process | Where-Object { $_.CPU -gt 10 } | Select-Object Name, CPU, Memory | Export-Csv "C:\Reports\ServerPerformance.csv" -NoTypeInformation
```

2. Users: For auditing or managing user information, `Get-ADUser` can pull information about Active Directory users, such as login times, group memberships, and account status. This can be customized to include the exact fields needed for a report.

Example: To generate a report of all users in a specific OU with details like account status and last login time:

```powershell
Get-ADUser -Filter * -SearchBase "OU=Employees,DC=domain,DC=com" -Properties Name, Enabled, LastLogonDate | Select-Object Name, Enabled, LastLogonDate | Export-Csv "C:\Reports\UserReport.csv" -NoTypeInformation
```

3. Network Devices: When managing network devices or configurations, `Get-NetAdapter`, `Get-NetIPAddress`, or `Get-NetRoute` can be used to gather details like IP configurations, interfaces, and routing tables. These can be compiled into a detailed report for network auditing or troubleshooting.

Example: To gather network adapter information for all devices and export it to a CSV:

```powershell
Get-NetAdapter | Select-Object Name, Status, MacAddress | Export-Csv "C:\Reports\NetworkDevices.csv" -NoTypeInformation
```

Exporting Reports to CSV, HTML, or PDF Format

Once your report is ready, PowerShell provides several options for exporting data into different formats, allowing easy sharing, visualization, or archiving.

1. CSV: CSV files are one of the most commonly used formats for exporting data, particularly because they are compatible with spreadsheet software like Excel. It's easy to create a report and export it using the `Export-Csv` cmdlet.

Example:

```powershell
Get-Process | Select-Object Name, CPU, Memory | Export-Csv "C:\Reports\ProcessReport.csv" -NoTypeInformation
```

2. HTML: If you need to create a more visually appealing report, HTML format allows you to add structure and styling. You can convert your PowerShell output to HTML using the `ConvertTo-Html` cmdlet. This is especially useful for creating reports that will be shared via web-based platforms or require enhanced readability.

Example:

```powershell
Get-Service | ConvertTo-Html -Property Name, Status | Out-File "C:\Reports\ServiceReport.html"
```

3. PDF: While PowerShell doesn't have a built-in cmdlet to export directly to PDF, there are third-party libraries like `PSWritePDF` or `Out-Printer` that you can use to generate PDF reports. Alternatively, you can first export the report to HTML or CSV and then convert it to PDF using external tools like Adobe Acrobat.

Example (using `PSWritePDF`):

```powershell
Get-Service | Select-Object Name, Status | Export-PSWritePDF -Path "C:\Reports\ServiceReport.pdf"
```

Generating reports is an essential function for IT administrators to ensure that their systems, users, and network devices are performing optimally and in compliance with organizational policies. PowerShell makes it easy to pull detailed information from various parts of your infrastructure and format it into reports that are both meaningful and shareable. Whether you're generating reports for servers, users, or network devices, PowerShell's flexibility and variety of export options allow you to create reports that fit your needs, in CSV, HTML, or PDF formats. By automating these tasks, you can save time, reduce errors, and enhance your ability to monitor and maintain IT environments efficiently.

Audit Logs and Security Monitoring

Using PowerShell to Query Security Logs and Perform Audits

PowerShell provides a powerful way to monitor and audit your systems by allowing you to query security logs, track activity, and analyze critical system events. By leveraging cmdlets like `Get-WinEvent`, `Get-EventLog`, and `Get-Content`, you can query Windows Event Logs, including security logs, to track activities such as login attempts, access control changes, and application errors. Security monitoring through PowerShell not only helps in ensuring compliance but also provides a proactive approach to identifying and addressing potential security threats before they escalate.

1. **Querying Security Logs:** To start auditing your system, you can use the `Get-WinEvent` cmdlet, which

is highly versatile for querying Windows Event Logs. To specifically target security-related events, you can filter based on Event IDs that correspond to security logs (such as login attempts, user privilege changes, or audit success/failure events).

Example: Querying failed logon attempts (Event ID 4625):

```powershell
Get-WinEvent -LogName Security -FilterXPath "*[System[EventID=4625]]" | Select-Object TimeCreated, Message | Export-Csv "C:\Reports\FailedLoginAttempts.csv" -NoTypeInformation
```

This command will search the Security log for failed login attempts (Event ID 4625) and export the details to a CSV file. You can adjust the Event ID to capture different types of events like successful logons (Event ID 4624) or account lockouts (Event ID 4740).

2. Tracking User Activity: By querying the security log for login events, user account modifications, or permission changes, you can track specific user actions on the system. This is crucial for compliance auditing and tracking malicious activities or unauthorized access.

Example: Tracking user logins (Event ID 4624):

```powershell
Get-WinEvent -LogName Security -FilterXPath "*[System[EventID=4624]]" | Select-Object TimeCreated, @{Name="UserName";Expression={$_.Properties[5].Value}} | Export-Csv "C:\Reports\UserLogins.csv" -NoTypeInformation
```

This query will capture successful login events, showing the user's name and the time they logged in.

3. Querying Failed Processes and System Events:
Failed processes, services, or system errors are logged in the Event Viewer and can be critical to troubleshoot potential security threats. You can use `Get-WinEvent` to capture error events, such as application crashes, failed service startups, or system misconfigurations.

Example: Querying application errors (Event ID 1000):

```powershell
Get-WinEvent -LogName Application -FilterXPath "*[System[EventID=1000]]" | Select-Object TimeCreated, Message | Export-Csv "C:\Reports\ApplicationErrors.csv" -NoTypeInformation
```

Tracking User Activity, Login Attempts, and Failed Processes

PowerShell can help you track user activity, login attempts, and failed processes through security logs, helping to ensure the security and integrity of your systems. By automating the collection of these events, you can monitor for unusual activity, failed login attempts, or system errors that could indicate malicious behavior or performance issues.

1. Tracking Login Attempts: Login attempts (both successful and failed) can provide insights into unauthorized access attempts, brute-force attacks, or legitimate access issues. Security logs with Event IDs 4624 (successful logins) and 4625 (failed logins) contain all the necessary data for tracking login activity. By regularly querying these logs, you can identify trends, such as frequent failed login attempts or unusual login times.

Example: To generate a daily report of failed logins:

```powershell
Get-WinEvent -LogName Security -FilterXPath "*[System[EventID=4625]]" | Where-Object { $_.TimeCreated -gt (Get-Date).AddDays(-1) } | Select-Object TimeCreated, @{Name="UserName";Expression={$_.Properties[5].Value}}, Message | Export-Csv "C:\Reports\FailedLogins_Daily.csv" -NoTypeInformation
```

This script filters for failed login events in the last 24 hours and exports them to a CSV file for review.

2. Tracking Failed Processes: Failed processes can often be a sign of misconfigurations or security issues. When critical processes fail, it may indicate potential attacks or system vulnerabilities that need immediate attention. You can monitor for these errors using

`Get-WinEvent` and filtering for application errors or critical system events.

Example: To track failed processes, particularly those that involve system services:

```powershell
Get-WinEvent -LogName System -FilterXPath "*[System[EventID=7000]]" | Select-Object TimeCreated, Message | Export-Csv "C:\Reports\FailedProcesses.csv" -NoTypeInformation
```

Event ID 7000 corresponds to service startup failures. By monitoring this event, you can proactively address service failures before they cause system downtime.

Using PowerShell to query security logs and track critical system events is a proactive approach to safeguarding your IT infrastructure. PowerShell allows you to automate the collection of security logs, track user activity, monitor login attempts, and audit system errors. By leveraging built-in cmdlets such as `Get-WinEvent`, `Get-EventLog`, and `Get-Content`, IT administrators can quickly identify potential security threats, monitor for unusual activity, and ensure that systems remain secure and compliant with organizational policies.

Automating these audit tasks with PowerShell can save significant time and resources, enabling you to quickly respond to security incidents, track changes, and generate reports for compliance purposes. With PowerShell's extensive capabilities, administrators can maintain a proactive security posture by continuously monitoring their systems and responding to potential issues before they escalate into serious threats.

Performance and Health Reports

Automating the Generation of System Health and Performance Reports

In an enterprise IT environment, maintaining system performance and health is essential for ensuring the availability and efficiency of critical services. One of the most powerful ways to achieve this is by automating the generation of system health and performance reports using PowerShell. These reports can provide valuable insights into the current status of your servers, applications, and overall infrastructure, helping you identify potential issues before they escalate into significant problems.

1. Generating System Health Reports: PowerShell's ability to interact with the system at a granular level allows you to capture detailed data about system health. Using cmdlets such as `Get-Process`, `Get-Service`, `Get-EventLog`, and performance counters, you can gather real-time data on various system resources, including CPU, memory, disk space, and network activity.

Example: Collecting a health report on system processes and services:

```powershell
$report = @()
  $report += Get-Process | Select-Object Name, CPU, Id, @{Name="Memory";Expression={[math]::round($_.WorkingSet / 1MB, 2)}}
  $report += Get-Service | Where-Object { $_.Status -eq 'Running' } | Select-Object Name, Status, StartType
  $report += Get-EventLog -LogName System -EntryType Error -Newest 10 | Select-Object TimeGenerated, Message

               $report         |         Export-Csv "C:\Reports\SystemHealthReport.csv" -NoTypeInformation
```

In this example, the script pulls data on running processes, active services, and recent system errors, then exports this information into a CSV file for easy review. The output is a comprehensive snapshot of the system's current health.

2. Performance Metrics and Trends: In addition to collecting static data, PowerShell can be used to generate ongoing performance reports by capturing performance counters. These counters track real-time data such as CPU usage, memory consumption, disk I/O, and network traffic. By regularly collecting this data, you can track trends over time and identify performance bottlenecks.

Example: Collecting performance data using performance counters:

```powershell
$cpuUsage = Get-Counter '\Processor(_Total)\% Processor Time'
$memUsage = Get-Counter '\Memory\Available MBytes'
$diskUsage = Get-Counter '\LogicalDisk(_Total)\% Free Space'

$report = [PSCustomObject]@{
    TimeStamp = Get-Date
    CPU_Usage = $cpuUsage.CounterSamples[0].CookedValue
    Mem_Available = $memUsage.CounterSamples[0].CookedValue
    Disk_Free_Space = $diskUsage.CounterSamples[0].CookedValue
}

$report | Export-Csv "C:\Reports\PerformanceReport.csv" -Append -NoTypeInformation
```

This script collects CPU, memory, and disk performance metrics and appends the data to a CSV file. The use of performance counters helps track resource usage in real-time, which is critical for identifying and troubleshooting performance issues.

Creating Alerts for Critical Thresholds and Automated Responses

In a production environment, performance issues can arise unexpectedly and may need immediate attention to avoid downtime or degraded service quality. One way to ensure that critical performance issues are identified early is by setting up alerts based on specific thresholds. These alerts notify administrators when a critical condition, such as high CPU usage or low disk space, occurs. PowerShell enables you to create these alerts and take automated actions in response to them.

1. Setting Thresholds for Alerts: PowerShell allows you to compare real-time performance data against predefined thresholds. If the system exceeds a threshold, you can trigger a custom action, such as sending an email, logging an event, or initiating a remediation script. This can be done through a combination of `if` statements and PowerShell cmdlets.

Example: Creating a CPU usage alert:

```powershell
$cpuUsage = Get-Counter '\Processor(_Total)\% Processor Time'
if ($cpuUsage.CounterSamples[0].CookedValue -gt 85) {
    Send-MailMessage -From "admin@domain.com" -To "it-support@domain.com" -Subject "Critical CPU Usage Alert" -Body "CPU usage is above 85%. Current value: $($cpuUsage.CounterSamples[0].CookedValue)%." -SmtpServer "smtp.domain.com"
}
```

This script checks if the CPU usage exceeds 85% and sends an email alert if the threshold is breached. By automating this process, administrators can immediately respond to performance issues without manual intervention.

2. Automating Remediation Actions: In some cases, the appropriate response to an alert might be an automated remediation action. For example, if disk space falls below a critical threshold, you can create a script that cleans up temporary files or expands disk volumes automatically. By automating these responses, you reduce the time required to address performance issues and prevent potential downtime.

Example: Automating disk space remediation:

```powershell
$diskUsage = Get-Counter '\LogicalDisk(_Total)\% Free Space'
if ($diskUsage.CounterSamples[0].CookedValue -lt 15) {
    # Clean up temporary files
    Remove-Item "C:\Temp\*" -Force
    # Send an email notification
    Send-MailMessage -From "admin@domain.com" -To "it-support@domain.com" -Subject "Disk Space Alert" -Body "Disk space is below 15%. Temporary files have been deleted." -SmtpServer "smtp.domain.com"
}
```

This script monitors disk space and automatically deletes temporary files if free space falls below 15%, helping to free up space and avoid disk-related performance issues.

Automating the generation of system health and performance reports is a powerful way to maintain the reliability and efficiency of your IT infrastructure. By leveraging PowerShell to collect detailed data, track performance trends, and generate customized reports, you can gain valuable insights into the health of your systems and identify potential issues before they cause significant disruptions. Moreover, creating alerts for critical thresholds and automating responses to performance issues ensures that your environment remains stable and secure, with minimal manual intervention required. Through these automated solutions, IT administrators can proactively manage their infrastructure, improving efficiency and reducing downtime while keeping systems running smoothly.

Scheduled Reports

Setting Up Scheduled Tasks to Automatically Generate and Send Reports

In an IT environment, staying on top of system health, performance metrics, and security logs is essential, but it can be time-consuming to manually run reports at regular intervals. This is where scheduled tasks come in. With PowerShell, you can automate the generation and delivery of reports on a set schedule, ensuring that critical information is always available when you need it without requiring any manual effort.

By leveraging PowerShell's `Task Scheduler` integration, you can configure scheduled tasks to run PowerShell scripts at defined intervals. These tasks can generate reports and even email them to administrators or save them to a network location for further review.

Let's break down the process for setting up scheduled reports:

1. Creating the PowerShell Script for Report Generation

Before scheduling a task, you'll need a PowerShell script that generates the report. This script could collect system health information, performance data, or audit logs. The following example generates a simple system health report.

Example script:

```powershell
$report = @()
$report += Get-Process | Select-Object Name, CPU, Id, @{Name="Memory";Expression={[math]::round($_.WorkingSet / 1MB, 2)}}
$report += Get-Service | Where-Object { $_.Status -eq 'Running' } | Select-Object Name, Status, StartType
$report += Get-EventLog -LogName System -EntryType Error -Newest 10 | Select-Object TimeGenerated, Message

$report | Export-Csv "C:\Reports\SystemHealthReport_$(Get-Date -Format 'yyyy-MM-dd').csv" -NoTypeInformation
```

This script collects the latest system processes, running services, and system errors, then exports the data to a CSV file with a date-specific filename.

2. Creating a Scheduled Task to Run the Script

After you have the script ready, the next step is to schedule it to run automatically at defined intervals. PowerShell allows you to use the `New-ScheduledTask` cmdlet to create scheduled tasks. Below is an example of how to create a scheduled task that runs the PowerShell script every day at 2:00 AM.

Example PowerShell code to schedule the task:

```powershell
$Action = New-ScheduledTaskAction -Execute "Powershell.exe" -Argument "-File C:\Scripts\GenerateSystemHealthReport.ps1"
$Trigger = New-ScheduledTaskTrigger -Daily -At "2:00AM"
$Principal = New-ScheduledTaskPrincipal -UserId "Administrator" -LogonType ServiceAccount
$Settings = New-ScheduledTaskSettingsSet -AllowStartIfOnBatteriesAreLow $true -StartWhenAvailable $true -DontStopIfGoingOnBatteries $true

Register-ScheduledTask -Action $Action -Trigger $Trigger -Principal $Principal -Settings $Settings -TaskName "Generate System Health Report"
```

This script does the following:
- Action: Specifies the PowerShell script to run (`GenerateSystemHealthReport.ps1`).

- Trigger: Sets the task to run daily at 2:00 AM.
- Principal: Defines the user account that the task will run under (Administrator).
- Settings: Ensures the task can run even if the machine is on battery power and attempts to start if the machine is not running at the scheduled time.

3. Sending the Reports Automatically via Email

For IT administrators, it's often more efficient to receive the reports via email rather than manually checking files. By incorporating PowerShell's `Send-MailMessage` cmdlet, you can automatically email the generated reports to the relevant parties.

Example code to send the report via email:

```powershell
$smtpServer = "smtp.domain.com"
$smtpFrom = "admin@domain.com"
$smtpTo = "it-support@domain.com"
$subject = "Daily System Health Report"
$body = "Please find attached the daily system health report."
$attachment = "C:\Reports\SystemHealthReport_$(Get-Date -Format 'yyyy-MM-dd').csv"

Send-MailMessage -From $smtpFrom -To $smtpTo -Subject $subject -Body $body -SmtpServer $smtpServer -Attachments $attachment
```

This script sends an email with the health report as an attachment. It dynamically pulls the file generated on the previous day, attaches it to the email, and sends it to the specified recipient.

4. Monitoring and Managing Scheduled Tasks

Once your scheduled task is set up, it's essential to monitor its performance and make sure it runs as expected. PowerShell provides several cmdlets for managing scheduled tasks, including `Get-ScheduledTask`, `Get-ScheduledTaskStatus`, and `Unregister-ScheduledTask`.

Example: Checking the status of the scheduled task:

```powershell
Get-ScheduledTask -TaskName "Generate System Health Report"
Get-ScheduledTaskStatus -TaskName "Generate System Health Report"
```

These cmdlets will return information about whether the task is enabled, when it was last run, and if there were any errors. This helps ensure that the scheduled report generation is functioning as planned.

Automating the generation and delivery of reports using scheduled tasks in PowerShell streamlines system monitoring and reporting, enabling IT teams to focus on higher-level priorities while ensuring that critical health and performance data is always up-to-date. With PowerShell, you can easily set up automated reports that are generated and delivered on a regular schedule, whether it's a daily system health report or a monthly performance review. By setting up these scheduled tasks, you save time, improve your workflow, and ensure that key stakeholders always have access to the latest insights without needing to manually run reports.

In this chapter, we've covered how to leverage PowerShell for creating custom reports and performing audits that are essential for maintaining an efficient and secure IT environment. From retrieving system logs to auditing Active Directory configurations, PowerShell offers a wide array of tools that allow for automated reporting, real-time monitoring, and compliance checks. By implementing the techniques discussed in this chapter, IT professionals can ensure they stay ahead of potential issues, improve system visibility, and foster a proactive approach to IT management. Armed with these reporting and auditing skills, you'll be able to better manage, monitor, and safeguard your systems.

Chapter 7

PowerShell Best Practices for IT Operations

PowerShell is a powerful tool for automating and managing IT tasks, but with great power comes great responsibility. As IT professionals, it's essential to not only understand how to use PowerShell but also to apply best practices that ensure scripts are efficient, secure, and maintainable. Whether you're managing servers, automating routine maintenance, or troubleshooting issues, adhering to best practices can help you avoid common pitfalls and enhance the reliability and performance of your IT operations.

In this chapter, we will explore key PowerShell best practices that will elevate your scripts and workflows. We'll cover strategies for writing clean and maintainable code, optimizing performance, securing your scripts, and ensuring that your automated tasks are robust and scalable. These practices will help you avoid errors, ensure security, and ultimately create more efficient and reliable IT solutions using PowerShell.

Writing Clean and Maintainable Scripts

In the world of IT automation, writing scripts that are not only functional but also clean, maintainable, and scalable is crucial. Clean code is easy to read, understand, and modify, which is especially important when working in team environments or maintaining scripts over time. As IT environments grow in complexity, it becomes essential to adhere to best practices that improve script readability, facilitate collaboration, and simplify future updates.

Code Structure, Comments, and Naming Conventions

1. **Organizing Code:** Well-structured scripts help developers and administrators understand the purpose and flow of the code. Break your code into logical sections with clear headers, and ensure that each section performs a distinct function.
    - Consistent Formatting: Use consistent indentation (typically 4 spaces per indent) to make the structure of your script clear. Align parameters and arguments within functions to make them easy to scan visually.

- Readable Blocks of Code: Organize your code into manageable blocks that perform one task at a time. Avoid large chunks of code that do too many things, as they become difficult to debug and understand.

2. **Comments:** Comments should explain why a particular approach is taken rather than how it works, which should be evident from the code itself. Clear and concise comments:
    - Explain complex logic or functions.
    - Provide context for decisions that might not be immediately obvious.
    - Mark TODOs and placeholders for areas that need further attention or optimization.

Example:

```powershell
    # Get list of all users in the HR department
    # Filters out users who have been inactive for more than 90 days
    $inactiveUsers = Get-ADUser -Filter * -SearchBase "OU=HR,DC=domain,DC=com" | Where-Object { $_.LastLogonDate -lt (Get-Date).AddDays(-90) }
```

3. Naming Conventions: Consistent and descriptive names for variables, functions, and parameters improve readability.
- Variables: Use camelCase for variables and parameters (e.g., `$serverName`, `$userCount`).
- Functions: Function names should use PascalCase, which is typically reserved for function names in PowerShell (e.g., `Get-UserInfo`, `Send-Alert`).
- Avoid Abbreviations: Unless commonly accepted (e.g., "IP" for Internet Protocol), avoid abbreviations that can be ambiguous.
- Use Descriptive Names: Choose names that describe the variable or function's role in the script. For example, instead of using `$x` or `$temp`, use `$filePath` or `$diskSpace`.

4. Consistency: Be consistent in how you name things, structure your scripts, and comment. For example, if you're using `Get-` as a prefix for function names (like `Get-UserInfo`), ensure that other similar functions follow the same naming pattern (e.g., `Get-FileDetails` instead of just `FileDetails`).

Script Modularity and Reusability

1. **Modular Scripts:** Instead of writing large monolithic scripts, break them into smaller, modular functions that can be reused across different projects. Each function should have one well-defined task. This approach improves maintainability because if a function needs to be updated, it's isolated to that function alone.

Example:

```powershell
# Function to get user details
Function Get-UserDetails {
    param ($username)
    Get-ADUser -Identity $username
}

# Function to generate a report
Function Generate-UserReport {
    param ($userDetails)
            $userDetails | Export-Csv "user_report.csv"
}
```

2. **Reuse Existing Functions**: Instead of rewriting functionality, take advantage of built-in cmdlets and functions that are already available in PowerShell, such as `Get-Process`, `Get-Service`, `Get-EventLog`, and

many others. This minimizes code duplication and ensures you are leveraging tested, optimized functions that work across various environments.

3. **Parameterization:** Use parameters in your functions to make them more flexible and reusable. Parameters allow your functions to accept inputs, making it easy to reuse the same script for different scenarios.

Example:

```powershell
Function Get-UserDetails {
   param (
     [string]$username,
               [string]$domain = 'defaultdomain.com'
   )
             Get-ADUser -Identity $username -Server $domain
}
```

4. **Error Handling:** Incorporate error handling into your functions so that they gracefully handle issues and provide meaningful feedback. This improves the robustness and reliability of your code. Use `Try`,

`Catch`, and `Finally` blocks to manage potential errors.

Example:

```powershell
Try {
    # Attempt to retrieve user details
    Get-ADUser -Identity $username
}
Catch {
        Write-Error "Failed to retrieve user: $username"
}
Finally {
        Write-Host "Function execution completed."
}
```

5. Use of Modules: Organize your reusable functions into PowerShell modules, which make it easier to distribute and maintain them. A module is a package of cmdlets, functions, variables, and workflows, and you can import it into any script or session. This is particularly useful for large-scale automation tasks that need to be reused across multiple systems or projects.

6. Documentation: Include a brief description of each function and what it does, as well as its parameters and expected output. PowerShell's built-in `Get-Help` functionality can be used to display this information, making it easier for others (or your future self) to understand and use the script.

Example:

```powershell
Function Get-UserDetails {
  <#
  .SYNOPSIS
     Retrieves the details of a specified Active Directory user.

  .PARAMETER username
     The username of the user whose details need to be retrieved.

  .EXAMPLE
  Get-UserDetails -username "johndoe"
  #>
  param (
    [string]$username
  )
  Get-ADUser -Identity $username
}
```

By following these guidelines, you'll be able to write scripts that are not only functional but also clean, maintainable, and adaptable to changing environments. Script modularity and reusability will help you automate IT tasks efficiently and with less chance of introducing errors. Whether you are working on a small one-time task or a large, ongoing automation project, the goal is to write code that is easy to understand, maintain, and improve over time.

Using Version Control for Scripts

Version control is a critical aspect of modern software development and IT automation, and it can significantly enhance your script management and collaboration. When working with PowerShell scripts, especially in larger teams or on long-term projects, version control systems (VCS) like Git provide a robust framework for tracking changes, managing different script versions, and collaborating effectively with other team members. Version control ensures that you have a history of script changes, can revert to previous versions when needed, and reduces the risk of losing important updates or configurations.

Best Practices for Managing PowerShell Scripts with Git or Other Version Control Systems

1. Use a Dedicated Repository for PowerShell Scripts
- Create a Repository: Set up a Git repository (using platforms like GitHub, GitLab, or Bitbucket) specifically for managing your PowerShell scripts. This ensures that all related scripts, modules, and configuration files are stored in a centralized location.
- Organize Your Repository: Use folders to organize your scripts by categories such as automation tasks, troubleshooting, AD management, etc. This will help keep the repository clean and easy to navigate.
- Example:

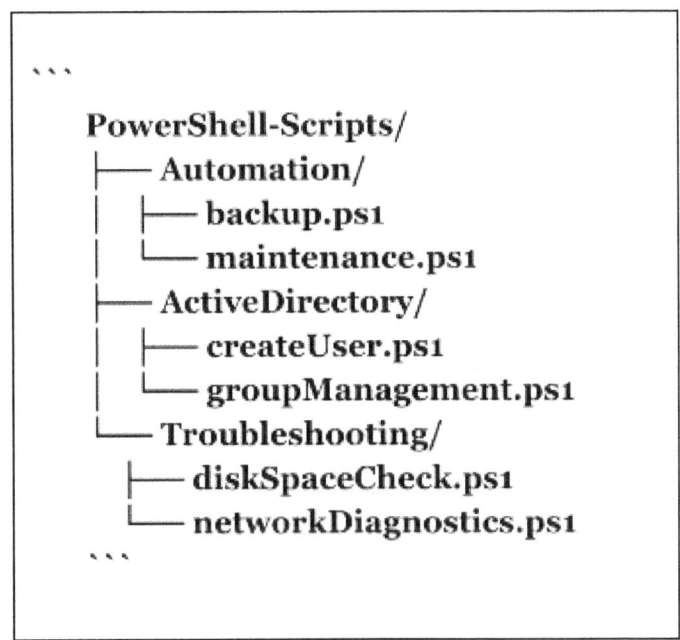

2. Commit Frequently with Meaningful Commit Messages

- Frequent Commits: Commit your changes regularly to keep track of incremental progress. This allows you to have a clear history of updates and changes. Each commit should represent a logical unit of work, such as adding a new feature, fixing a bug, or refactoring code.
- Descriptive Commit Messages: Write clear and meaningful commit messages that explain *what* was changed and *why* the change was necessary. This will help you and your team understand the context of the change at a glance.

Example commit messages:
- `Added function to check disk space on remote servers`
- `Refactored user creation script for better readability`
- `Fixed issue with date formatting in backup report`

3. Branching and Merging
- Use Feature Branches: When working on new features or large changes, create a new branch to isolate your work from the main branch (usually `main` or `master`). This allows you to experiment with changes without affecting the stability of the main codebase.
- Merge Changes: Once your feature or bug fix is complete, merge it back into the main branch. Always test the changes thoroughly before merging to ensure that the script is still working as intended.

4. Avoid Storing Sensitive Information
- Exclude Sensitive Files: Never store sensitive data such as passwords, API keys, or configuration files with sensitive information directly in the repository. Use `.gitignore` to prevent sensitive files from being added to the version control system.

- Use Secrets Management: For sensitive data, utilize PowerShell's native secrets management features or store sensitive information in secure vaults (e.g., Azure Key Vault) and reference it securely within your scripts.

5. Collaborating with Others
- Pull Requests: If you're working in a team, use pull requests (PRs) to review and discuss changes before merging them into the main branch. PRs are a great way to get feedback on your code, catch potential issues early, and ensure that your changes align with project standards.
- Code Reviews: Encourage code reviews as part of your version control process. This practice allows other team members to review your changes, spot potential issues, and suggest improvements. It also ensures that multiple sets of eyes are looking at the code, reducing the likelihood of bugs or inefficiencies.

6. Tagging and Releases
- Tag Releases: When a script or module is stable and ready for deployment, tag it with a version number (e.g., `v1.0`, `v1.1`) to mark milestones or releases. This makes it easy to track and reference stable versions of the code.
- Semantic Versioning: Use semantic versioning (e.g., `1.0.0`) to denote major, minor, and patch

updates, which can help differentiate between large, breaking changes and small incremental improvements.

7. **Using Git with PowerShell Scripts**
   - Integrating with PowerShell: Git can be used directly within PowerShell scripts or from the PowerShell command line. For example, you can automate version control tasks using Git commands inside your PowerShell scripts:

```powershell
git status
git add .
git commit -m "Updated script for performance monitoring"
git push origin main
```

8. **Tracking Changes and History**
   - Reviewing History: Git allows you to view the entire history of your script, making it easy to track when changes were made and by whom. You can use `git log` to view commit history and `git diff` to compare changes between commits.

Example:

```powershell
git log --oneline
git diff HEAD~1
```

- Reverting Changes: If a change causes issues, you can easily revert to a previous version of the script using Git commands like `git checkout` or `git revert`. This makes it much easier to recover from mistakes and minimize downtime.

Example:
```powershell
git checkout HEAD~1 script.ps1
```

9. **Automating Deployment with Git**
    - Continuous Integration/Continuous Deployment (CI/CD): If you are working in a more complex environment, you may want to automate the deployment of PowerShell scripts. Tools like Jenkins, Azure DevOps, or GitLab CI/CD can be configured to automatically deploy scripts from the Git repository to servers or systems whenever

changes are made. This ensures that your scripts are always up-to-date and available across your infrastructure.

10. Using Git Hooks
- Pre-commit Hooks: Git hooks are scripts that run automatically at certain points in the Git workflow, such as before committing or before pushing. You can use pre-commit hooks to enforce best practices, such as checking for syntax errors, running tests, or ensuring that commit messages follow a particular format.

By following these best practices for using version control with PowerShell scripts, you can improve collaboration, ensure consistency, and streamline the management of your IT automation efforts. Version control will also help you track the evolution of your scripts, roll back changes when necessary, and keep your work organized as your automation environment grows.

Error Handling and Debugging

In IT automation, the ability to efficiently handle errors and debug PowerShell scripts is crucial for ensuring smooth, reliable operations. Errors are inevitable, but how they are managed can make the difference between a script that fails silently and one that provides useful feedback, allowing you to quickly identify and resolve issues. Proper error handling can also help in creating more robust automation scripts, enabling them to gracefully handle unexpected conditions without disrupting the entire workflow.

Debugging, on the other hand, is about identifying and correcting mistakes or unexpected behavior in your code. PowerShell provides several tools and techniques that you can use to troubleshoot and resolve issues in your scripts, from simple syntax errors to complex runtime exceptions.

Advanced Error Handling Strategies and Logging

PowerShell's error handling system provides various ways to manage errors, from simple try-catch blocks to more sophisticated logging and custom error handling mechanisms. Here's how you can leverage these features:

1. Using Try, Catch, and Finally Blocks
- Try Block: The `try` block is used to execute commands that might generate an error. If an

error occurs in the `try` block, PowerShell will immediately jump to the `catch` block.
- Catch Block: The `catch` block handles the error. It allows you to define how to respond to specific types of errors.
- Finally Block: The `finally` block runs code that should execute regardless of whether an error occurred or not (e.g., cleanup operations).

Example:

```powershell
try {
    # Attempt to copy a file
    Copy-Item "C:\source\file.txt" "C:\destination\file.txt"
}
catch {
    Write-Error "An error occurred while copying the file: $_"
}
finally {
    Write-Host "File copy operation complete."
}
```

2. Using Error Action Preferences

- PowerShell allows you to control the behavior of error handling using the `-ErrorAction` parameter. The following values are useful:
    - `Stop`: Immediately stops execution and triggers the `catch` block.
    - `Continue`: Default behavior, continues execution and writes a non-terminating error message.
    - `SilentlyContinue`: Hides error messages.
    - `Inquire`: Prompts for user input on how to handle the error.

Example:

```powershell
Get-Content "C:\nonexistentfile.txt" -ErrorAction Stop
```

3. **Logging Errors for Troubleshooting**
    - Logging errors is critical for long-running scripts and automated jobs. By saving error details to a log file, you can later analyze and diagnose the issue.
    - You can use `Start-Transcript` to capture output, including errors, to a file:

```powershell
Start-Transcript -Path "C:\Logs\PowerShellScript.log"
try {
    # Code that may throw an error
}
catch {
    Write-Error "Error: $_"
}
Stop-Transcript
```

4. **Using `$Error` and `$LastExitCode`**
   - The `$Error` automatic variable stores a collection of errors that occurred during the session. You can access it to retrieve detailed information about the last error.
   - `$LastExitCode` provides the exit code of the last Windows command or process executed.

Example:
```powershell
if ($Error.Count -gt 0) {
    Write-Host "Last error message: $($Error[0].Exception.Message)"
}
```

5. **Throwing Custom Errors**
    - Sometimes you may want to throw your own errors when certain conditions are met in your script. You can use `throw` to generate a custom error.

Example:
```powershell
if (-not (Test-Path "C:\importantfile.txt")) {
    throw "The required file was not found!"
}
```

Debugging Techniques for Complex PowerShell Scripts

When your scripts become more complex, it's essential to have the right tools and techniques to troubleshoot them. PowerShell offers several debugging methods that can make identifying and resolving issues more manageable:

1. Using the PowerShell Debugger

- PowerShell includes an interactive debugger that allows you to pause execution and inspect variables and the call stack.
- You can enable the debugger by using the `Set-PSDebug` cmdlet:

```powershell
Set-PSDebug -Trace 1
```

This will display each command as it is executed, making it easier to identify where errors are occurring.

- To step through a script line-by-line, use the `-Step` option:

```powershell
Set-PSDebug -Step
```

2. Using Breakpoints
- You can set breakpoints in your script to stop execution at a specific point. This allows you to inspect the state of variables, run commands interactively, and step through the script.

- Use the `Set-PSBreakpoint` cmdlet to set a breakpoint:

```powershell
Set-PSBreakpoint -Script "C:\Scripts\MyScript.ps1" -Line 15
```

To remove a breakpoint:

```powershell
Remove-PSBreakpoint -Breakpoint 1
```

3. **Verbose and Debug Output**
   - PowerShell has two built-in output streams that help with debugging: `Write-Verbose` and `Write-Debug`.
   - `Write-Verbose` allows you to print messages only when the `-Verbose` flag is used.
   - `Write-Debug` prints messages only when the `-Debug` flag is used.

Example:

```powershell
Write-Verbose "This is a verbose message"
Write-Debug "This is a debug message"
```

4. Using the `$Debug` Variable
- The `$Debug` variable can be set to `true` to enable debug output, helping you troubleshoot the script in more detail.

Example:
```powershell
$DebugPreference = "Continue"
```

5. Inspecting Variables and Objects
- During debugging, inspecting variables and objects at runtime is essential. Use `Get-Member` to explore the properties and methods of objects:

```powershell
$process = Get-Process -Name "explorer"
$process | Get-Member
```

6. Trace-Command for Detailed Tracking

- The `Trace-Command` cmdlet allows you to trace specific events during script execution, such as function calls or variable accesses.

Example:

```powershell
Trace-Command -Name CommandDiscovery -Expression { Get-Process } -PSHost
```

7. Error Handling with `Trap`

- The `trap` statement is a legacy error handling mechanism in PowerShell, which is useful in specific scenarios but is not recommended for modern scripts. When an error occurs in the `try` block, control is passed to the `trap` block.

Example:

```powershell
trap {
    Write-Host "Error caught: $($_.Exception.Message)"
    continue
}
```

By mastering these error handling and debugging strategies, you'll be able to create more reliable and maintainable PowerShell scripts. Whether you're automating administrative tasks or troubleshooting complex issues, these techniques will help you address problems quickly and efficiently, ensuring that your scripts can handle unexpected situations and continue running smoothly in production environments.

Optimizing PowerShell Scripts for Performance

In the world of IT automation and system management, performance is paramount. As scripts grow in complexity, it becomes increasingly important to ensure that they execute quickly, efficiently, and with minimal resource usage. A slow or inefficient PowerShell script can lead to delays in critical tasks, strain on system resources, and longer processing times, all of which can hinder productivity and increase costs.

Optimizing your PowerShell scripts for performance ensures that they run as efficiently as possible, especially when automating large-scale tasks like managing multiple servers, querying large datasets, or handling multiple user accounts. In this section, we'll explore key performance considerations, best practices for writing optimized scripts, and methods for reducing resource usage to maximize efficiency.

Performance Considerations and Best Practices for Efficient Script Execution

PowerShell is a powerful scripting language, but if used incorrectly, it can consume excessive memory and CPU cycles. Here are several key performance considerations and best practices for writing more efficient PowerShell scripts:

1. Avoiding Unnecessary Loops
- Loops are a common source of performance bottlenecks, especially when they involve large datasets. It's essential to evaluate whether a loop

is necessary or if there's a more efficient method to achieve the same result.

For example, instead of looping through a list of items to process each one, consider using built-in cmdlets like `Where-Object` or `Select-Object` that can perform filtering or selection more efficiently.

```powershell
# Inefficient loop
$items = Get-Item "C:\Files\*"
foreach ($item in $items) {
  if ($item.Extension -eq ".txt") {
    Write-Host $item.Name
  }
}

# More efficient alternative
Get-Item "C:\Files\*" | Where-Object { $_.Extension -eq ".txt" } | ForEach-Object { Write-Host $_.Name }
```

2. Using `Where-Object` and `ForEach-Object` Efficiently
- While `Where-Object` and `ForEach-Object` are useful cmdlets, they can also cause performance issues when not used properly. Avoid unnecessary

use of `Where-Object` in a loop when you can filter the collection before the loop.

For instance:

```powershell
# Inefficient
$files = Get-ChildItem "C:\path\to\dir" | Where-Object { $_.Extension -eq ".txt" }

# More efficient
$files = Get-ChildItem "C:\path\to\dir" -Filter "*.txt"
```

3. Using `Select-Object` Instead of Creating Large Arrays
- Avoid creating large arrays in memory when you only need to work with a subset of properties or objects. `Select-Object` allows you to select only the properties you need, improving both performance and memory consumption.

Example:

```powershell
# Inefficient (creating large array in memory)
$allUsers = Get-ADUser -Filter * | Select-Object Name, Department, EmailAddress, Manager

# More efficient (selecting only the properties needed)
$users = Get-ADUser -Filter * -Properties Name, Department, EmailAddress, Manager | Select-Object Name, EmailAddress
```

4. Limiting Remote Commands

- When working with remote systems, try to minimize the number of remote calls. Each remote call adds overhead, and excessive remote operations can slow down the execution of your scripts.

For example, instead of running the same command on multiple remote systems individually, you can execute commands in parallel or batch them together to reduce the time spent waiting for responses.

```powershell
# Inefficient (one call at a time)
    Invoke-Command -ComputerName Server1 -ScriptBlock { Get-Process }
    Invoke-Command -ComputerName Server2 -ScriptBlock { Get-Process }

# More efficient (running commands in parallel)
$computers = "Server1", "Server2"
$computers | ForEach-Object {
    Invoke-Command -ComputerName $_ -ScriptBlock { Get-Process }
}
```

Minimizing Memory Usage and Optimizing Loops and Queries

Memory management is another critical aspect of script performance. While PowerShell automatically handles some memory management tasks, it's still possible to optimize your scripts to minimize memory usage, particularly when working with large datasets or when running scripts in long-duration jobs.

1. Using `-Filter` and `-SearchBase` for Optimized Queries

- When querying Active Directory, file systems, or databases, use the `-Filter` parameter whenever possible to limit the amount of data retrieved. This reduces memory usage and speeds up the query.

Example:

```powershell
# Inefficient query (retrieving all users)
$users = Get-ADUser -Filter * -Properties *

# Optimized query (retrieving only needed properties)
$users = Get-ADUser -Filter { Enabled -eq $true } -Properties Name, Department
```

2. Releasing Unused Variables and Objects
- After performing operations on large objects or datasets, be sure to release memory by setting variables to `$null` when they are no longer needed. PowerShell uses garbage collection, but manually clearing variables can sometimes improve memory management, especially for large scripts.

```powershell
$largeDataSet = Get-Data
# Process large dataset
$largeDataSet = $null   # Release memory
```

3. **Efficient Use of Loops**
    - Loops are an essential part of automation, but inefficient loops can dramatically impact performance. Consider the following tips to optimize loops:
    - Use `ForEach-Object` for pipeline operations to process objects one at a time, rather than creating large in-memory arrays.
    - Avoid nested loops where possible, as they can lead to excessive CPU usage and slower script performance.
    - Limit the number of iterations by filtering data early, so you don't process unnecessary objects.

Example of optimizing a loop:

```powershell
# Inefficient (nested loop)
foreach ($user in $users) {
  foreach ($group in $groups) {
    if ($user.Group -eq $group.Name) {
      Write-Host "$($user.Name) belongs to $($group.Name)"
    }
  }
}

# Optimized (using hash table for direct lookup)
$groupDict = @{}
  foreach ($group in $groups) { $groupDict[$group.Name] = $group }

foreach ($user in $users) {
  if ($groupDict.ContainsKey($user.Group)) {
    Write-Host "$($user.Name) belongs to $($user.Group)"
  }
}
```

4. Leveraging Pipelining for Memory Efficiency

- PowerShell's pipeline allows data to be passed from one cmdlet to the next without holding everything in memory. This is particularly useful when processing large amounts of data.
- Use cmdlets like `Select-Object`, `Where-Object`, and `Sort-Object` to filter and process data in the pipeline, rather than creating large intermediate objects in memory.

Example:

```powershell
# Inefficient (storing all results in memory)
$allFiles = Get-ChildItem "C:\Logs\*" -Recurse | Where-Object { $_.Extension -eq ".log" }

# Optimized (using pipeline)
Get-ChildItem "C:\Logs\*" -Recurse | Where-Object { $_.Extension -eq ".log" } | ForEach-Object { $_.Name }
```

5. Parallel Processing with `ForEach-Object -Parallel`
- PowerShell 7 introduced the ability to run tasks in parallel within the `ForEach-Object` cmdlet using the `-Parallel` parameter. This can be extremely useful for scripts that need to run the same operation on multiple machines or items concurrently, drastically reducing execution time.

Example:

```powershell
$computers = @("Server1", "Server2", "Server3")
$computers | ForEach-Object -Parallel {
    Invoke-Command -ComputerName $_ -ScriptBlock { Get-Process }
}
```

Optimizing PowerShell scripts for performance is a combination of strategic design, efficient coding practices, and smart resource management. By following these best practices—avoiding unnecessary loops, optimizing queries, minimizing memory usage, and leveraging parallel processing—you can ensure that your scripts run faster, use fewer resources, and scale better in production environments. With these techniques, you'll be able to create automation solutions that are both effective and efficient, allowing you to get the most out of your PowerShell scripts while maintaining system performance and reliability.

By applying the best practices outlined in this chapter, you can ensure that your PowerShell scripts and automations are both effective and sustainable. From writing efficient, reusable code to maintaining security standards, these guidelines are designed to help you make the most of PowerShell in your IT operations. Adopting these practices will not only improve your workflows and performance but will also empower you to tackle complex IT challenges with confidence, knowing that you're following proven, best-in-class methodologies. PowerShell is a tool for efficiency, but using it correctly will ensure that your IT environment remains secure, scalable, and optimized for success.

Chapter 8

Advanced PowerShell Techniques and Automation

As you become proficient with PowerShell, you'll start to see its vast potential for automation and complex problem-solving. While the fundamentals will take you far, mastering advanced PowerShell techniques will allow you to tackle more sophisticated IT tasks, manage larger environments, and build highly efficient automation solutions. This chapter will introduce advanced concepts that will elevate your PowerShell skills, including working with PowerShell modules, automating remote management, and leveraging advanced scripting patterns. Whether you're managing hundreds of servers or automating intricate workflows, these techniques will provide you with the tools necessary to scale your PowerShell knowledge and enhance your IT operations.

PowerShell Remoting

PowerShell remoting is one of the most powerful features of PowerShell, enabling administrators to manage remote systems with ease. It eliminates the need for direct physical or remote desktop access to each machine, allowing you to execute commands and run scripts across multiple computers or servers simultaneously. In this section, we will explore how to enable and use PowerShell remoting to manage remote systems, and how to execute commands and scripts remotely using cmdlets like `Invoke-Command` and `Enter-PSSession`.

Enabling PowerShell Remoting

Before you can use PowerShell remoting, it must be enabled on the remote systems you intend to manage. By default, remoting is disabled for security reasons. To enable PowerShell remoting on a machine, you can use the `Enable-PSRemoting` cmdlet, which configures the system to accept remote commands over PowerShell. This cmdlet is typically run on the target system:

```powershell
Enable-PSRemoting
-Force
```

This command configures the system to listen for incoming remoting requests, sets up firewall exceptions, and configures necessary services (like WinRM) to ensure remote access. After enabling remoting, PowerShell remoting should be ready for use, provided that the user has appropriate permissions and that any firewalls or network settings allow remoting traffic.

Executing Remote Commands with `Invoke-Command`

Once remoting is enabled, you can execute commands on remote systems using the `Invoke-Command` cmdlet. This allows you to run a single command or a block of commands on one or more remote machines. Here's an example of how to use `Invoke-Command`:

```powershell
Invoke-Command -ComputerName RemotePC -ScriptBlock { Get-Process }
```

In this example, the `Invoke-Command` cmdlet is used to retrieve a list of running processes from a remote machine named `RemotePC`. The `-ScriptBlock` parameter specifies the block of code that will be executed remotely.

You can also use `Invoke-Command` to run a script on multiple remote computers simultaneously:

```powershell
Invoke-Command -ComputerName RemotePC1, RemotePC2 -ScriptBlock { Get-Process }
```

This command will execute the same script on both `RemotePC1` and `RemotePC2` in parallel, providing an efficient way to run commands across multiple systems at once.

Interactive Remote Sessions with `Enter-PSSession`

For more interactive, real-time management, the `Enter-PSSession` cmdlet allows you to establish a persistent remote session with a remote system. Once connected, you can interact with the remote system as if you were working locally, typing commands and receiving immediate responses. To start an interactive session with a remote computer:

```powershell
Enter-PSSession -ComputerName RemotePC
```

Once the session is established, your prompt changes to reflect the remote session, and you can run any commands interactively. To exit the session, use the `Exit-PSSession` cmdlet:

```powershell
Exit-PSSession
```

This is particularly useful when you need to troubleshoot or manage a system interactively but don't want to physically access the machine.

Running Scripts Remotely

PowerShell remoting isn't limited to simple commands. You can also run full PowerShell scripts on remote systems. For example, you can copy a script to a remote system using `Copy-Item` or create and execute a script block on the fly:

```powershell
Invoke-Command -ComputerName RemotePC -ScriptBlock {
    C:\Scripts\MyScript.ps1
}
```

This command remotely runs a script located at `C:\Scripts\MyScript.ps1` on `RemotePC`. PowerShell remoting is smart enough to handle running these scripts, even if they are complex and involve multiple commands or parameters.

Credential Management for Remoting

In some cases, you may need to provide credentials for the remote system. PowerShell allows you to supply credentials securely using the `-Credential` parameter. For example:

```powershell
$cred = Get-Credential
Invoke-Command
-ComputerName RemotePC
-Credential $cred
-ScriptBlock { Get-Service }
```

In this example, the `Get-Credential` cmdlet prompts you to enter credentials, which are then used for the remote command execution. This ensures that you can securely access remote systems without storing sensitive passwords in your scripts.

Using Remoting Across Multiple Systems

PowerShell remoting is especially powerful in larger environments where you need to perform the same task on multiple systems. The `Invoke-Command` cmdlet can target multiple remote computers, enabling batch operations without the need for interactive logins. For instance, to check disk space across a fleet of servers:

```powershell
$servers = @("Server1", "Server2", "Server3")
Invoke-Command -ComputerName $servers -ScriptBlock { Get-PSDrive }
```

This command runs `Get-PSDrive` across all three servers simultaneously, providing a snapshot of the drive information for each one. This ability to target multiple machines at once is invaluable for system administrators managing large infrastructures.

In conclusion, PowerShell remoting is an essential tool for managing systems across multiple computers, automating administrative tasks, and troubleshooting in real-time. By mastering the `Invoke-Command`, `Enter-PSSession`, and credential management techniques, you can streamline operations and improve efficiency in managing remote systems. Whether you are performing routine maintenance, troubleshooting, or executing complex scripts, PowerShell remoting can dramatically enhance your ability to manage and automate IT tasks at scale.

Managing Cloud Resources with PowerShell

As cloud computing becomes increasingly integral to modern IT infrastructure, managing cloud resources efficiently has become a critical skill for IT professionals. Whether you are working with Microsoft Azure, Amazon Web Services (AWS), or other cloud environments, PowerShell provides robust modules that enable you to automate, manage, and interact with these cloud platforms directly from the command line. In this section, we'll explore how to use PowerShell to manage cloud resources, automate cloud infrastructure tasks, and simplify cloud-based operations.

Managing Cloud Resources with PowerShell Modules

Each major cloud platform—such as Azure, AWS, and Google Cloud—has its own PowerShell module designed to interact with their respective services. These modules allow you to automate cloud-based tasks like provisioning virtual machines, managing storage accounts, and handling networking configurations, all from within PowerShell.

Azure PowerShell

Azure PowerShell is a powerful tool that helps you manage Microsoft Azure resources. With Azure PowerShell, you can automate the provisioning of virtual machines, configure networks, and manage other Azure services. To use Azure PowerShell, you need to first install the `Az` module, which is the unified module for managing Azure resources.

Installing the Azure PowerShell Module:

```powershell
Install-Module -Name Az -AllowClobber -Force
```

Once installed, you can connect to your Azure account using:

```powershell
Connect-AzAccount
```

After authenticating, you can manage Azure resources like virtual machines, storage accounts, and networks using cmdlets like `New-AzVM`, `Get-AzStorageAccount`, and `Set-AzVirtualNetwork`.

Example - Creating a Virtual Machine in Azure:

```powershell
New-AzVM -ResourceGroupName "MyResourceGroup" -Location "EastUS" -VMName "MyVM" -ImageName "UbuntuLTS" -Size "Standard_B1s"
```

This command provisions a new virtual machine in the "EastUS" region with the Ubuntu image.

AWS PowerShell

The AWS Tools for PowerShell allow you to manage AWS services such as EC2 instances, S3 buckets, and RDS databases. These tools are available through the AWS PowerShell module, which can be installed using the `Install-Module` cmdlet.

Installing the AWS PowerShell Module:

```powershell
Install-Module -Name AWSPowerShell
```

After installation, you can authenticate with your AWS account:

```powershell
Set-AWSCredential -AccessKey YOUR_ACCESS_KEY -SecretKey YOUR_SECRET_KEY -Region us-east-1
```

Once connected, you can automate the management of AWS services. For example, to create a new EC2 instance, you can use the `New-EC2Instance` cmdlet:

Example - Launching an EC2 Instance:

```powershell
New-EC2Instance -ImageId ami-0abcdef1234567890 -InstanceType t2.micro -KeyName MyKeyPair -MinCount 1 -MaxCount 1
```

This will create a new EC2 instance in AWS using the specified image ID and instance type.

Google Cloud PowerShell

Google Cloud also supports PowerShell through the `GoogleCloud` module, which you can use to manage resources like virtual machines, storage, and databases.

Installing the Google Cloud PowerShell Module:

```powershell
Install-Module -Name GoogleCloud
```

After installation, authenticate to your Google Cloud account using the following:

```powershell
gcloud auth login
```

Once authenticated, you can use PowerShell cmdlets to interact with Google Cloud resources. For example, to list virtual machine instances:

```powershell
Get-GceInstance
```

This will return all virtual machines in your Google Cloud environment.

Automating Cloud Infrastructure Tasks

PowerShell is particularly effective for automating cloud infrastructure tasks, such as the creation of virtual machines, management of storage accounts, and configuring networking. By leveraging the power of cloud APIs, you can easily automate repetitive tasks and integrate cloud management into your IT operations.

Creating Virtual Machines

In both Azure and AWS, you can automate the process of creating and configuring virtual machines with just a few lines of PowerShell. These tasks typically involve specifying the region, operating system image, size of the VM, and other configurations.

Automating VM Creation in Azure:

```powershell
New-AzVM -ResourceGroupName "MyResourceGroup" -Location "EastUS" -VMName "MyVM" -ImageName "UbuntuLTS" -Size "Standard_B1s" -VirtualNetworkId "/subscriptions/{subscriptionId}/resourceGroups/{resourceGroup}/providers/Microsoft.Network/virtualNetworks/{vnetName}"
```

This script creates a virtual machine in Azure with a specified virtual network.

Automating VM Creation in AWS:

```powershell
New-EC2Instance -ImageId ami-0abcdef1234567890 -InstanceType t2.micro -KeyName MyKeyPair -MinCount 1 -MaxCount 1
```

The above PowerShell script automates the launch of an EC2 instance in AWS, saving you time compared to manually provisioning each instance.

Managing Cloud Storage

PowerShell can also be used to automate the management of cloud storage resources. In Azure, AWS, and Google Cloud, you can create, manage, and delete storage accounts, upload and download files, and even automate backups and archiving.

Automating Storage Management in Azure:

```powershell
New-AzStorageAccount -ResourceGroupName "MyResourceGroup" -Location "EastUS" -StorageAccountName "mystorageaccount" -SkuName Standard_LRS -Kind StorageV2
```

This creates a new Azure storage account with the specified parameters.

Automating Storage Management in AWS:

```powershell
New-S3Bucket -BucketName "my-aws-bucket"
```

This creates a new S3 bucket in AWS to store your files.

Managing Cloud Networking

In addition to virtual machines and storage, PowerShell can also help automate cloud networking tasks, such as configuring virtual networks, subnets, and security groups. For example, you can automate the creation of a virtual network in Azure or the configuration of a security group in AWS.

Creating a Virtual Network in Azure:

```powershell
New-AzVirtualNetwork -ResourceGroupName "MyResourceGroup" -Location "EastUS" -Name "MyVNet" -AddressPrefix "10.0.0.0/16"
```

Creating a Security Group in AWS:

```powershell
New-EC2SecurityGroup -GroupName "MySecurityGroup" -Description "Security group for EC2 instances"
```

Best Practices for Managing Cloud Resources with PowerShell

- Automate Repetitive Tasks: Automate common tasks like VM provisioning, storage management,

and security configurations to save time and reduce human error.
- Secure Cloud Credentials: Always use secure methods to store and retrieve credentials, such as environment variables or Azure Key Vault/AWS Secrets Manager.
- Use Templates for Consistency: Use templates or predefined scripts to ensure consistency in cloud resource provisioning across different environments.

Managing cloud resources with PowerShell allows IT administrators to automate and streamline the deployment and management of virtual machines, storage, and networking across various cloud environments. Whether you're working with Azure, AWS, or Google Cloud, PowerShell offers powerful tools to create, manage, and automate cloud infrastructure tasks, making it a crucial skill for modern IT operations. By mastering these techniques, you can enhance your cloud management processes, reduce administrative overhead, and ensure the efficiency and scalability of your cloud-based infrastructure.

Building Custom PowerShell Modules

Custom PowerShell modules allow IT professionals to encapsulate reusable functions and scripts into portable, manageable packages. These modules can standardize processes, simplify task execution, and improve collaboration across teams by providing a consistent set of tools. In this section, we'll explore how to create, package, distribute, and import custom PowerShell modules for your organization.

Creating Your Own Reusable PowerShell Modules

A PowerShell module is essentially a collection of functions and scripts stored in a single directory. Modules can include advanced features like metadata, help documentation, and nested modules.

Steps to Create a PowerShell Module

1. Define the Purpose of Your Module:
   Identify the tasks your module will perform and the functions it will contain. Group related functions together for clarity and efficiency.

2. Create a Directory for the Module:
   Name the directory after your module (e.g., `MyModule`). This will be the container for your module files.

```powershell
New-Item -ItemType Directory -Path "$env:USERPROFILE\Documents\WindowsPowerShell\Modules\MyModule"
```

3. *Write the Functions:*

Create a `.psm1` file (PowerShell module script) that contains the functions. Save it in the module directory.

Example `MyModule.psm1`:

```powershell
function Get-CustomGreeting {
  param ([string]$Name)
    "Hello, $Name! Welcome to PowerShell modules."
}

function Get-CurrentTime {
  Get-Date
}
```

4. *Create a Manifest File:*

The manifest file (`.psd1`) provides metadata about your module, such as its version, author, and exported functions.

Example `MyModule.psd1`:

```powershell
@{
    ModuleVersion = '1.0.0'
    Author = 'Your Name'
    Description = 'A custom PowerShell module for example purposes.'
    FunctionsToExport = @('Get-CustomGreeting', 'Get-CurrentTime')
    NestedModules = @()
}
```

Generate a manifest using the `New-ModuleManifest` cmdlet:

```powershell
New-ModuleManifest -Path "$env:USERPROFILE\Documents\WindowsPowerShell\Modules\MyModule\MyModule.psd1" -RootModule "MyModule.psm1" -FunctionsToExport Get-CustomGreeting,Get-CurrentTime -Description "A custom PowerShell module."
```

Packaging and Distributing Custom Modules

Packaging and distributing PowerShell modules ensure that others can easily install and use them within your organization.

Packaging Your Module
Ensure your module directory contains:
- The `.psm1` file with your functions.
- The `.psd1` manifest file for metadata.

Compress the directory into a `.zip` file if distributing manually or use a version control system like Git for team-wide access.

Publishing to a Central Repository

For larger organizations or public distribution, publish your module to a repository like PowerShell Gallery or an internal NuGet repository.

Publishing to PowerShell Gallery:

1. Create a free account on [PowerShell Gallery](https://www.powershellgallery.com/).
2. Install the `PowerShellGet` module if not already installed.
3. Package your module into a `.nupkg` file using `Save-Module`:

```powershell
Save-Module -Name MyModule -Path C:\Modules
```

4. Publish the module:

```powershell
Publish-Module -Path C:\Modules\MyModule -NuGetApiKey <YourAPIKey>
```

Importing and Using Custom Modules

Once a module is distributed, it can be imported and used on other systems.

Installing a Module
If the module is shared manually, place it in the correct module directory:
- User-specific location: `` `$env:USERPROFILE\Documents\WindowsPowerShell\Modules` ``
- System-wide location: `` `C:\Program Files\WindowsPowerShell\Modules` ``

For published modules, use:

```powershell
Install-Module -Name MyModule
```

Importing a Module
To use the module in a PowerShell session:

```powershell
Import-Module -Name MyModule
```

Using Module Functions
After importing, call the functions in the module:

```powershell
Get-CustomGreeting -Name "Alice"
Get-CurrentTime
```

Best Practices for Custom Modules

1. Consistent Naming:

Use clear, descriptive names for functions and modules. Follow verb-noun conventions (e.g., `Get-`, `Set-`, `Remove-`).

2. Documentation:

Include help information for each function using comment-based help and a comprehensive `README` file.

Example comment-based help:

```powershell
<#
.SYNOPSIS
Generates a custom greeting.

.PARAMETER Name
The name to include in the greeting.

.EXAMPLE
Get-CustomGreeting -Name "Alice"
#>
```

3. Testing:

Test modules thoroughly in different environments to ensure compatibility.

4. Versioning:

Use semantic versioning (e.g., 1.0.0) to track changes and updates to your module.

5. Security:

Avoid hardcoding sensitive data. Use secure methods like environment variables or credential objects.

Building custom PowerShell modules enables IT professionals to create standardized, reusable tools for their teams. Whether for internal automation, team collaboration, or public distribution, modules encapsulate the power of PowerShell in a structured, maintainable way. By mastering the creation, packaging, and distribution of modules, you can greatly enhance your efficiency and scalability in managing IT operations and beyond.

Using PowerShell with APIs and Web Services

In modern IT operations, interacting with APIs (Application Programming Interfaces) and web services is an essential skill. PowerShell provides powerful tools to automate and simplify these interactions, making it easier to work with cloud platforms, third-party services, and internal systems that expose data via APIs. This section will cover how to use PowerShell to work with REST APIs, handle JSON data, and make HTTP requests to retrieve or send data.

Working with REST APIs and JSON Data in PowerShell

REST (Representational State Transfer) APIs are one of the most common ways to interact with external systems and services. PowerShell provides native cmdlets that make it easy to query and consume RESTful APIs, handle the response data, and integrate it into your automation workflows.

Basics of Working with REST APIs

APIs typically return data in JSON format, which is easy to parse and manipulate. PowerShell's `Invoke-RestMethod` and `Invoke-WebRequest` cmdlets are designed to interact with REST APIs, each serving different purposes but often used interchangeably depending on the situation.

- `Invoke-RestMethod`: This cmdlet is best suited for working with RESTful APIs that return data, especially JSON. It simplifies parsing and handling responses.

- `Invoke-WebRequest`: While this cmdlet also makes HTTP requests, it returns more detailed information, including headers and raw content, which can be useful for troubleshooting or for APIs that don't return JSON data.

Making a Basic API Request

To make a simple API request using `Invoke-RestMethod`, you need the URL of the API endpoint and possibly an authentication token (if required).

Example: *GET Request to an API*

Let's say you want to retrieve a list of users from a REST API endpoint:

```powershell
$response = Invoke-RestMethod -Uri "https://api.example.com/users" -Method Get
$response
```

In this example:
- `-Uri` specifies the API endpoint.
- `-Method Get` defines the HTTP method to be used, in this case, a GET request to retrieve data.

The response from the API will typically be returned as a PowerShell object, where each JSON object is converted into properties you can access.

Making a POST Request to Send Data

In addition to retrieving data, you may also need to send data to an API, which is commonly done using a POST request. This is useful for actions like creating new records, updating resources, or triggering workflows.

Example: *POST Request with JSON Data*

```powershell
# Prepare the data you want to send
$data = @{
    Name = "John Doe"
    Email = "johndoe@example.com"
} | ConvertTo-Json

# Send a POST request with JSON payload
$response = Invoke-RestMethod -Uri "https://api.example.com/users" -Method Post -Body $data -ContentType "application/json"
$response
```

- `ConvertTo-Json` converts the PowerShell object into JSON format.
- `-Body` passes the JSON data to the API.
- `-ContentType` specifies the content type (in this case, `application/json`).

Handling Authentication

Many APIs require authentication via API keys or OAuth tokens. These are usually passed in the HTTP headers for security reasons.

Example: *GET Request with Authentication Header*

```powershell
# Define your API key or token
$headers = @{
  "Authorization" = "Bearer YOUR_API_TOKEN"
}

# Send the request with the authorization header
$response = Invoke-RestMethod -Uri "https://api.example.com/protected" -Method Get -Headers $headers
$response
```

- Authorization: Most APIs use a token-based authentication system (such as OAuth2), which requires including the token in the `Authorization` header.

Handling Responses in PowerShell

Once you receive the response from an API, it typically returns data in JSON format. PowerShell automatically converts the JSON data into objects, making it easy to work with.

Parsing JSON Data

Once the response is stored in a variable (e.g., `$response`), you can access its properties directly.

For example, if the API response contains user details:

```powershell
$response = Invoke-RestMethod -Uri "https://api.example.com/users" -Method Get

# Access specific user properties
$response.users | ForEach-Object {
    Write-Host "User Name: $_.Name, User Email: $_.Email"
}
```

- In this case, `$response.users` represents an array of user objects returned by the API. You can iterate over the array with `ForEach-Object` and display user names and emails.

Error Handling and Response Validation

It's important to handle any errors that may occur during the request. PowerShell allows you to handle HTTP status codes and exceptions effectively.

```powershell
try {
        $response = Invoke-RestMethod -Uri "https://api.example.com/data" -Method Get
    if ($response -eq $null) {
        Write-Host "No data returned from the API."
    } else {
       Write-Host "API Response: $response"
    }
} catch {
   Write-Host "An error occurred: $_"
}
```

- `try/catch` blocks catch any exceptions thrown during the request, allowing you to handle unexpected errors.
- You can also check for empty responses or specific HTTP status codes to validate the data received.

Advanced Usage: Handling Complex APIs

Some APIs may return more complex data, include pagination for large datasets, or require additional headers or parameters. PowerShell gives you full flexibility to handle such cases.

Working with Pagination

If an API returns data in pages (e.g., a large list of users), you need to loop through multiple requests until all data is retrieved. This can be done using a `while` loop.

Example: Handling Pagination

```powershell
$uri = "https://api.example.com/users"
$allUsers = @()
$page = 1

while ($true) {
        $response = Invoke-RestMethod -Uri "$uri?page=$page" -Method Get
   $allUsers += $response.users
   if ($response.hasMorePages -eq $false) { break }
   $page++
}

$allUsers
```

In this example:
- The script continuously fetches pages of users from the API, adding them to `$allUsers` until no more pages are available.

PowerShell makes it easy to interact with APIs, handle HTTP requests, and manage data returned from web services. With `Invoke-RestMethod` and `Invoke-WebRequest`, you can integrate external systems into your IT automation workflows, retrieve real-time data, and create powerful, automated solutions. Whether it's querying cloud services, gathering system metrics, or integrating third-party tools, PowerShell's ability to work with APIs opens up limitless possibilities for streamlining your IT processes and enhancing efficiency.

The advanced techniques covered in this chapter are designed to push the boundaries of your PowerShell capabilities. With a deeper understanding of automation, remote management, and advanced scripting patterns, you'll be able to create robust, scalable solutions to even the most complex IT challenges. By applying these methods, you can streamline repetitive tasks, manage large-scale infrastructures, and create flexible scripts that adapt to a variety of environments and use cases. Mastering these advanced skills not only makes you a more efficient IT professional but also sets you apart as a true PowerShell expert capable of driving significant improvements in automation and operations management.

Chapter 9

Real-World Case Studies and Examples

While learning PowerShell's syntax, cmdlets, and core concepts is essential, the true power of automation and scripting comes to life when you apply these skills to real-world IT challenges. In this chapter, we'll explore practical case studies and examples that demonstrate how PowerShell is used to solve common and complex IT problems. From automating daily administrative tasks to troubleshooting critical server issues and managing large infrastructures, these case studies will illustrate how PowerShell's versatility can streamline operations, improve efficiency, and reduce human error in IT environments. By examining these real-world scenarios, you'll gain actionable insights and be able to adapt these solutions to your own organization.

Case Study 1: Automating Daily IT Maintenance

Overview:

IT administrators often spend a significant amount of time performing routine maintenance tasks such as checking server health, applying system updates, monitoring disk space, and verifying system backups. These tasks, while essential, are often repetitive and time-consuming. By automating them using PowerShell, administrators can save time, reduce errors, and ensure that systems are always in optimal condition without the need for constant manual intervention.

The Problem:

The organization in this case study, a mid-sized enterprise, faced the challenge of manually performing daily maintenance on a fleet of Windows servers. IT staff were responsible for tasks such as:

- Checking system health (CPU usage, memory utilization, disk space).
- Ensuring that operating system patches and updates were applied.
- Verifying that backups were completed successfully.
- Monitoring and managing antivirus software updates.

These tasks were time-consuming and error-prone when done manually, often leading to missed steps or delayed responses to critical issues. Furthermore, as the organization grew, the number of servers and systems that needed to be checked daily increased, putting additional strain on the IT team.

The PowerShell Solution:

The solution was to automate these tasks using PowerShell scripts that ran on a scheduled basis, significantly reducing manual labor and improving operational efficiency.

Script Components:

1. System Health Checks:
- A PowerShell script was created to check key performance metrics of the servers, including:
- CPU usage (`Get-WmiObject Win32_Processor`).
- Memory utilization (`Get-WmiObject Win32_OperatingSystem`).
- Disk space (`Get-PSDrive`).
- The script would send alerts via email if any metrics exceeded predefined thresholds (e.g., CPU usage over 90%, disk space under 10%).

2. Automated Updates:

- The script used `Get-WindowsUpdate` (or a similar cmdlet for patch management) to check for available Windows updates.
- Updates were applied automatically during off-hours to minimize disruptions, and results were logged for auditing purposes.

3. Backup Verification:
- A portion of the script checked the status of backup jobs by querying the backup software's logs or checking the backup folder for the presence of recent backup files.
- Alerts were triggered if the script detected any issues, such as a missed or failed backup.

4. Antivirus Update Checks:
- The script queried the antivirus software's status using PowerShell commands specific to the software (e.g., `Get-MpComputerStatus` for Windows Defender).
- Alerts were sent if the antivirus definitions were out of date or if the antivirus software was disabled.

Execution:

- The script was saved as a `.ps1` file and scheduled to run automatically each day using the Windows Task Scheduler.

- The PowerShell script would run in the background, gathering the necessary system information and performing the maintenance tasks at specified times, without requiring manual intervention.
- Results were logged to a central location and email notifications were sent if there were any issues or actions taken (e.g., updates applied, backups successful, or resource thresholds exceeded).

Results and Benefits:

By automating daily maintenance tasks with PowerShell, the organization realized several key benefits:

1. Time Savings:
- IT staff no longer needed to manually check each server every day. The automation freed up time to focus on more strategic projects and troubleshooting high-priority issues.

2. Improved System Health:
- Regular health checks and automated updates ensured that systems remained up to date, reducing the risk of vulnerabilities and performance issues caused by outdated software.

3. **Reduced Errors:**
   - Automating the tasks minimized the risk of human error, such as forgetting to check certain servers, missing critical updates, or overlooking failed backups.

4. **Faster Response Times:**
   - With alerts and notifications, IT administrators were able to respond quickly to any issues, such as failing disk space or antivirus updates, before they became larger problems.

5. **Better Reporting and Auditing:**
   - The logs generated by the script provided a comprehensive report of the actions performed, which could be reviewed during audits or troubleshooting. The reports were also used for compliance purposes to ensure that the organization's systems met internal security standards.

By leveraging PowerShell to automate daily IT maintenance tasks, the organization significantly improved operational efficiency and reduced manual intervention. The IT team could focus on more impactful tasks while ensuring that systems remained secure, up-to-date, and healthy. This case study demonstrates how PowerShell can be a powerful tool for automating routine administrative work, ultimately saving time, improving system reliability, and enhancing overall productivity within an IT environment.

Case Study 2: Troubleshooting and Optimizing Server Performance

Overview:

Server performance issues can have a direct impact on business operations, leading to slow application response times, unresponsiveness, and potential downtime. In this case study, we'll walk through how PowerShell was used to diagnose and resolve a performance bottleneck on a production server, resulting in improved efficiency and system stability.

The Problem:

A large e-commerce company was experiencing performance issues on its primary production server, which was responsible for handling customer transactions and inventory updates. Customers reported slow page load times, and the server often experienced high CPU usage during peak hours. IT staff had tried basic troubleshooting steps (such as restarting services and checking resource usage in Task Manager), but the problem persisted.

Key symptoms of the issue included:

- High CPU utilization (over 85%) during peak times.
- Sluggish application performance (slow response times when accessing inventory data).
- Intermittent system freezes and application timeouts.
- An overall increase in customer complaints during busy shopping periods.

With the root cause unclear, the IT team needed a methodical and reliable way to identify and fix the issue without affecting service continuity.

The PowerShell Solution:

PowerShell was chosen as the tool to diagnose and resolve the server performance issue, primarily because of its powerful diagnostic cmdlets, ability to analyze detailed system metrics, and its scripting capabilities for automating fixes.

Step 1: Gathering System Performance Data

The first step in troubleshooting was to gather detailed performance data to identify the root cause of the issue.

CPU Usage:

Using the `Get-Process` cmdlet, the team identified that a specific application process (`WebApp.exe`) was consuming a disproportionate amount of CPU resources.

```powershell
Get-Process -Name WebApp | Select-Object Id, CPU, ProcessName
```

Memory Utilization:

The team then checked memory usage to determine if the issue was related to insufficient RAM or memory leaks.

```powershell
Get-Process | Sort-Object -Property WorkingSet -Descending | Select-Object -First 10 Id, ProcessName, WorkingSet
```

Disk Performance:

They used the `Get-Volume` and `Get-PSDrive` cmdlets to monitor disk usage and check if the disk I/O was contributing to the bottleneck.

```powershell
Get-PSDrive -PSProvider FileSystem
Get-Volume
```

Event Logs:

By querying the event logs for system errors, the team found warnings related to the application process, indicating that the app was failing to handle large requests, which led to timeouts and CPU spikes.

```powershell
Get-WinEvent -LogName System | Where-Object { $_.Message -like "*WebApp*" } | Select-Object TimeCreated, Message
```

Step 2: Identifying the Bottleneck

Based on the data collected, the team discovered that the `WebApp.exe` process was experiencing CPU spikes due to inefficient database queries. The queries were not properly indexed, causing excessive CPU usage when the application accessed the database.

The team also found that the server had insufficient free disk space, which was exacerbating the problem when the application tried to log data to disk.

Step 3: Resolving the Issue

Once the root causes were identified, the IT team used PowerShell to implement the following optimizations:

1. Terminating Unnecessary Processes:
They used PowerShell to terminate any unnecessary background processes that were consuming excessive CPU resources.

```powershell
Stop-Process -Name UnusedProcess -Force
```

2. Optimizing the Database:
The team created a script to monitor and optimize the SQL queries executed by `WebApp.exe`. They used

PowerShell to invoke SQL Server Management cmdlets and rebuild database indexes, which significantly reduced the query time and CPU consumption.

```powershell
Invoke-Sqlcmd -Query "ALTER INDEX ALL ON [Table] REBUILD" -ServerInstance "SQLServerName"
```

3. Clearing Temporary Files:

To free up disk space, the IT team created a PowerShell script to delete temporary files and clear out old log data from the disk.

```powershell
Remove-Item -Path "C:\Temp\*" -Recurse -Force
```

4. Scheduling Regular Disk Cleanups:

The team scheduled this cleanup task to run weekly using the `Task Scheduler`, ensuring that the disk would not fill up again.

```powershell
$Action = New-ScheduledTaskAction -Execute "PowerShell.exe" -Argument "C:\scripts\disk_cleanup.ps1"
$Trigger = New-ScheduledTaskTrigger -Daily -At "2:00AM"
Register-ScheduledTask -Action $Action -Trigger $Trigger -TaskName "Disk Cleanup" -Description "Cleanup temporary files"
```

5. Performance Monitoring:

They created a PowerShell script to monitor CPU usage every 15 minutes and send an email alert if the CPU usage exceeded 85%.

```powershell
$cpuUsage = (Get-WmiObject Win32_Processor | Select-Object -ExpandProperty LoadPercentage)
If ($cpuUsage -gt 85) {
    Send-MailMessage -To "admin@company.com" -Subject "High CPU Alert" -Body "CPU Usage is over 85% on ServerName." -SmtpServer "smtp.company.com"
}
```

Step 4: Testing and Validation

After implementing the fixes, the IT team tested the system to ensure that the issue had been resolved. They used PowerShell to perform stress tests on the server by simulating high traffic and monitoring resource utilization in real-time.

- The `Get-Process` cmdlet showed that CPU usage during peak load dropped significantly, and the server's disk usage was well below critical levels.
- The database optimizations resulted in faster query execution, and server health reports

confirmed that the system was now running efficiently.

Results and Benefits:

By leveraging PowerShell for troubleshooting and optimization, the IT team was able to:

1. Reduce CPU Usage:
The application's CPU usage dropped from over 85% to under 40%, even during peak traffic hours.

2. Improve Disk Health:
Disk usage dropped to healthy levels, with the disk cleanup scripts ensuring that the system maintained adequate free space.

3. Optimize Application Performance:
Optimizing the database queries significantly reduced server load, resulting in faster application performance and reduced application timeouts.

4. Automate Ongoing Monitoring:
Automated monitoring and alerts ensured that potential performance issues could be detected early and addressed before they impacted end-users.

5. Increase Server Uptime:

By resolving the underlying issues and automating maintenance tasks, the IT team improved server stability and uptime, reducing service disruptions.

This case study illustrates how PowerShell can be a valuable tool in diagnosing and resolving performance bottlenecks on production servers. By leveraging PowerShell's extensive command set, the IT team was able to pinpoint the root causes of the issue, optimize the system, and automate ongoing performance monitoring. As a result, the company experienced improved system performance, reduced downtime, and greater operational efficiency. This case underscores the power of PowerShell not only in troubleshooting but also in proactively maintaining and optimizing IT infrastructure.

Case Study 3: Managing Active Directory at Scale

Overview:

In large organizations, managing user accounts, groups, and permissions in Active Directory (AD) can become a daunting task. For companies with thousands of users and multiple departments, performing manual operations is inefficient, error-prone, and time-consuming. In this case study, we'll examine how PowerShell was used to automate and streamline bulk operations in Active Directory, helping an IT team manage thousands of user accounts efficiently.

The Problem:

A global financial services company with multiple offices around the world had grown its employee base to over 10,000 employees. Each employee required an Active Directory (AD) account, along with specific permissions based on their department and role. Managing these accounts manually or through traditional GUI-based methods had become impractical due to the size of the organization.

The key challenges the IT team faced included:

Onboarding and Offboarding Employees:
   The HR department provided daily lists of new hires and terminations. Managing these changes manually was time-consuming, and errors often occurred, leading to unnecessary administrative overhead.

Bulk Modifications:
   Employees' roles and department assignments frequently changed, requiring bulk updates to AD groups, permissions, and attributes (e.g., changing users' email addresses, titles, and phone numbers).

Account Auditing:

IT needed a reliable and scalable way to query AD for security audits, permissions reviews, and reporting, ensuring that users had the correct access.

The team needed a solution to handle these repetitive tasks efficiently while maintaining accuracy.

The PowerShell Solution:

PowerShell was selected as the ideal tool for managing Active Directory at scale, given its native support for AD management tasks through the `ActiveDirectory` module, which provides powerful cmdlets to create, modify, and query AD objects. PowerShell's ability to handle bulk operations in an automated fashion was key to improving efficiency and minimizing human error.

Step 1: Automating Onboarding and Offboarding

To address the onboarding and offboarding process, the IT team created a PowerShell script that automated user account creation and deletion based on a CSV file provided by HR. The script could create user accounts with the correct attributes, add them to the appropriate groups, and ensure their email addresses were properly configured.

Onboarding Script:

```powershell
$csv = Import-Csv -Path "C:\HR\NewHires.csv"
foreach ($user in $csv) {
    New-ADUser -SamAccountName $user.UserName
-UserPrincipalName $user.Email -Name $user.FullName `
        -GivenName $user.GivenName -Surname
$user.Surname -Department $user.Department `
        -Title $user.Title -PasswordNeverExpires $true
-Enabled $true
    Add-ADGroupMember -Identity $user.Department
-Members $user.UserName
}
```

This script read from a CSV file containing new employee data and created AD user accounts automatically, while adding them to the appropriate department groups. By automating this process, the IT team ensured that new employees were onboarded quickly and with minimal errors.

Offboarding Script:

```powershell
$csv = Import-Csv -Path "C:\HR\Terminations.csv"
foreach ($user in $csv) {
    Remove-ADUser -Identity $user.UserName -Confirm:$false
}
```

For offboarding, the script read a CSV file of terminated employees and automatically removed their AD accounts, ensuring that accounts were disabled or deleted without delay.

Step 2: Bulk Modifications of User Attributes

Employees often change departments or roles within the organization, necessitating bulk changes to their AD profiles. The IT team used PowerShell to update user attributes like department, email, and phone numbers, which were provided in CSV files.

Bulk Modification Script:

```powershell
$csv = Import-Csv -Path "C:\HR\RoleChanges.csv"
foreach ($user in $csv) {
    Set-ADUser -Identity $user.UserName -Department $user.NewDepartment -Title $user.NewTitle
    Set-ADUser -Identity $user.UserName -EmailAddress $user.NewEmail
}
```

This script made bulk updates to user accounts in AD, adjusting department names, job titles, and email addresses as needed, ensuring that all changes were made simultaneously and accurately.

Step 3: Automating Group Membership Management

Managing AD group memberships for thousands of users, especially during role transitions or when departments change, can be a complex task. The IT team created PowerShell scripts that could add and remove users from multiple groups at once based on their roles or department changes.

Managing Group Memberships:

```powershell
$csv = Import-Csv -Path "C:\HR\GroupChanges.csv"
foreach ($user in $csv) {
    Remove-ADGroupMember -Identity $user.OldGroup -Members $user.UserName
    Add-ADGroupMember -Identity $user.NewGroup -Members $user.UserName
}
```

This script was used to move users between groups when they changed departments, ensuring that their access and permissions were always up-to-date.

Step 4: Auditing Active Directory

With so many users and groups, auditing AD permissions and reviewing access was critical for maintaining security and compliance. PowerShell allowed the IT team to create comprehensive audit reports that tracked group memberships, permissions, and user activity.

Audit Script:

```powershell
Get-ADUser -Filter * | Select-Object SamAccountName, Name, Department, Title | Export-Csv -Path "C:\Reports\ADAuditReport.csv"
```

This script generated a full report of user accounts, including their department and title, which was then exported to CSV for review. The team could quickly analyze the data to ensure that users had the correct access levels.

Step 5: Scheduling and Automating Tasks

The IT team also leveraged Task Scheduler and PowerShell's ability to automate these scripts on a recurring basis. This ensured that tasks such as adding new users, removing terminated employees, and auditing group memberships were handled without manual intervention, further improving efficiency.

For example, the onboarding and offboarding scripts were scheduled to run daily at specific times, automatically processing the daily batch of new hires and terminations.

```powershell
$Action = New-ScheduledTaskAction -Execute "PowerShell.exe" -Argument "C:\scripts\onboarding.ps1"
$Trigger = New-ScheduledTaskTrigger -Daily -At "8:00AM"
Register-ScheduledTask -Action $Action -Trigger $Trigger -TaskName "User Onboarding" -Description "Automated user onboarding process"
```

Results and Benefits:

By using PowerShell to manage Active Directory at scale, the IT team was able to achieve the following:

1. Increased Efficiency:
Automation reduced the amount of manual work involved in creating and managing user accounts, cutting down processing times from hours to minutes.

2. Minimized Errors:

Automating the process reduced human error and ensured consistency across user accounts, groups, and permissions.

3. Improved Scalability:
The IT team could easily scale operations to handle the increasing number of employees, ensuring the process remained efficient as the company grew.

4. Faster Onboarding and Offboarding:
New hires were onboarded quickly, and terminations were processed immediately, reducing the risk of security breaches from lingering accounts.

5. Enhanced Compliance and Security:
Automated auditing ensured that the company remained compliant with internal security policies and external regulations, providing easy access to reports for security audits.

This case study demonstrates the power of PowerShell in managing Active Directory at scale. By automating bulk user creation, updates, and deletions, the IT team was able to streamline their processes, increase efficiency, and minimize errors. PowerShell's flexibility and automation capabilities proved to be invaluable in maintaining a secure and compliant environment as the company continued to grow. This case reinforces how powerful PowerShell can be in large-scale IT operations, particularly when managing user accounts, group memberships, and permissions across thousands of users.

Case Study 4: Reporting and Auditing in a Corporate Environment

Overview:

In a large corporate IT environment, maintaining security and operational efficiency requires constant monitoring, auditing, and reporting. With thousands of devices, servers, and user accounts to manage, performing these tasks manually is impractical. This case study explores how PowerShell was leveraged to automate the generation of real-time performance reports and security audits, allowing the IT team to proactively monitor and respond to system health and security concerns in real time.

The Problem:

A multinational corporation with hundreds of servers, workstations, and network devices required continuous monitoring and reporting to maintain optimal performance and ensure compliance with internal security policies. The IT team faced several challenges:

Real-Time Performance Monitoring:

The company's IT infrastructure was complex, with diverse systems running critical business operations. IT needed to quickly identify performance issues such as high CPU usage, low memory availability, or slow response times that could affect business operations.

Security Audits and Compliance:

Regular audits were necessary to track user activity, access to sensitive data, and other security metrics. Manual audits were time-consuming and often out-of-date by the time they were completed, leaving the company vulnerable to security risks.

Customized Reports:

Different departments required specific types of reports: system health reports for operations teams, security audits for compliance officers, and detailed performance reports for senior management. Generating these reports manually for each department was inefficient and prone to errors.

The company required an automated solution that would allow them to generate consistent, accurate, and real-time reports on system performance and security.

The PowerShell Solution:

The IT team turned to PowerShell, taking advantage of its powerful scripting capabilities and ease of automation. With PowerShell, the team was able to automate the collection and generation of reports that were tailored to the needs of each department, providing real-time data on system health, security, and performance.

Step 1: Real-Time Performance Reporting

The IT team needed to generate real-time performance reports for critical servers to ensure they were operating within acceptable thresholds. Using PowerShell, they created scripts that monitored various performance counters, such as CPU usage, memory utilization, disk space, and network throughput.

Performance Monitoring Script:

```powershell
$servers = @("Server1", "Server2", "Server3")
foreach ($server in $servers) {
    $cpu = Get-WmiObject -Class Win32_Processor -ComputerName $server | Select-Object -ExpandProperty LoadPercentage
    $memory = Get-WmiObject -Class Win32_OperatingSystem -ComputerName $server | Select-Object -ExpandProperty FreePhysicalMemory
    $disk = Get-WmiObject -Class Win32_LogicalDisk -ComputerName $server | Where-Object { $_.DriveType -eq 3 } | Select-Object DeviceID, @{Name="UsedSpace";Expression={($_.Size - $_.FreeSpace)/1GB}}, @{Name="FreeSpace";Expression={$_.FreeSpace/1GB}}
    $network = Get-WmiObject -Class Win32_NetworkAdapterConfiguration -ComputerName $server | Select-Object IPAddress, MACAddress

    # Export the data to a CSV file for reporting
    $report = [PSCustomObject]@{
        ServerName = $server
        CPUUsage = $cpu
        FreeMemoryGB = [math]::round($memory / 1MB, 2)
        DiskUsage = $disk
        NetworkInfo = $network
    }

    $report | Export-Csv -Path "C:\Reports\PerformanceReport.csv" -Append -Force
}
```

This script checks the CPU usage, free memory, disk space, and network adapter information for a list of servers. The data is then exported to a CSV file, which can be used by IT staff to quickly assess the health of servers in real time.

By automating performance checks, the team could respond to potential issues—such as disk space running low or a server's CPU reaching maximum capacity—before they escalated into problems that affected productivity.

Step 2: Security Audits and User Activity Reporting

Security audits were a critical component of the company's compliance efforts, especially for sensitive financial data and customer information. Using PowerShell, the IT team created scripts that tracked user login attempts, password changes, and access to critical resources.

Security Audit Script:

```powershell
$logs = Get-WinEvent -LogName Security -FilterXPath "*[System[EventID=4720 or EventID=4722 or EventID=4723]]" -MaxEvents 1000
foreach ($log in $logs) {
  $user = $log.Properties[0].Value
  $eventID = $log.Id
  $time = $log.TimeCreated
  $message = $log.Message

  # Export the audit data to a CSV file
  $auditReport = [PSCustomObject]@{
    User = $user
    EventID = $eventID
    Time = $time
    Message = $message
  }
                $auditReport | Export-Csv -Path "C:\Reports\SecurityAuditReport.csv" -Append -Force
}
```

This script queries the security event log to extract relevant events such as user account creation (EventID 4720), user account enabled (EventID 4722), and password changes (EventID 4723). The details, including the user involved, event time, and the event message, are then exported to a CSV file for compliance auditing.

By automating security audits, the IT team ensured that logs were collected and reports generated without manual intervention. This process also reduced the risk of missing important security events that could indicate potential threats.

Step 3: Custom Reports for Different Departments

The IT department was required to produce different types of reports for various internal stakeholders, including system administrators, management, and compliance officers. Using PowerShell, custom reports could be tailored to the specific needs of each department.

For example, the operations team required detailed server performance data, while compliance officers needed reports on security events. To streamline this, the IT team created modular scripts that could generate reports in CSV, HTML, or PDF formats based on user input.

Custom Reporting Script:

```powershell
$reportType = Read-Host "Enter report type (CSV, HTML, PDF)"

switch ($reportType) {
  "CSV" {
    # Generate CSV report
            $data | Export-Csv -Path "C:\Reports\CustomReport.csv" -NoTypeInformation
  }
  "HTML" {
    # Generate HTML report
            $data | ConvertTo-Html -Property ServerName, CPUUsage, FreeMemoryGB, DiskUsage | Out-File "C:\Reports\CustomReport.html"
  }
  "PDF" {
        # Generate PDF report (using external tools or libraries like `PSWritePDF`)
      $data | ConvertTo-Pdf -OutputPath "C:\Reports\CustomReport.pdf"
  }
}
```

This flexible script allowed the IT team to select the format required for the report, automating the creation of customized reports for various departments and stakeholders.

Step 4: Automating Report Distribution

Once reports were generated, they needed to be distributed to the relevant parties. PowerShell was used to automate the emailing of reports to stakeholders, ensuring that key team members always received the latest data.

Email Automation Script:

```powershell
$smtpServer = "smtp.company.com"
$emailFrom = "it-admin@company.com"
$emailTo = "management@company.com"
$subject = "Daily Performance Report"
$body = "Please find attached the daily performance report."

$mailmessage = New-Object system.net.mail.mailmessage
$mailmessage.from = ($emailFrom)
$mailmessage.To.Add($emailTo)
$mailmessage.Subject = $subject
$mailmessage.Body = $body
$mailmessage.Attachments.Add("C:\Reports\PerformanceReport.csv")

$smtp = New-Object Net.Mail.SmtpClient($smtpServer)
$smtp.Send($mailmessage)
```

This script automatically emailed the daily performance reports to management, with the report attached as a CSV file. By automating report distribution, the IT team ensured that management always had access to the most up-to-date data without requiring manual intervention.

Results and Benefits:

The use of PowerShell to automate reporting and auditing provided the company with several benefits:

1. Efficiency Gains:
Automated reporting saved significant time, enabling the IT team to focus on more strategic tasks rather than manually generating reports.

2. Real-Time Monitoring:
Real-time performance reports allowed the IT team to monitor server health and respond to potential issues before they impacted operations.

3. Improved Security Compliance:
Automated security audits helped ensure compliance with internal and external regulations, reducing the risk of security breaches.

4. Customizable Reports:
By using PowerShell to generate custom reports in multiple formats, the team could cater to the specific needs of different departments, ensuring stakeholders had the right information at the right time.

5. Proactive IT Operations:
The ability to automate performance monitoring, security audits, and report distribution enabled the IT team to be more proactive in managing the IT infrastructure, reducing downtime and improving overall system reliability.

PowerShell proved to be an invaluable tool for automating reporting and auditing in this large corporate IT environment. By automating performance monitoring, security audits, and the generation and distribution of custom reports, the IT team was able to streamline operations, improve system health, and ensure compliance. This case study highlights how PowerShell can be used to create a robust and efficient reporting framework, providing real-time insights and reducing the manual workload in large, complex IT environments.

The case studies presented in this chapter showcase the real-world potential of PowerShell for IT professionals, system administrators, and those looking to automate and optimize their IT workflows. Whether it's automating routine tasks, enhancing server management, or troubleshooting system failures, PowerShell is an indispensable tool in the modern IT toolkit. These examples serve as inspiration, showing how PowerShell can be leveraged to tackle common challenges and improve operational efficiency. By applying these strategies and adapting the solutions to your specific needs, you can take your PowerShell skills to the next level and harness the full potential of automation in your IT environment.

Chapter 10

Conclusion and Next Steps

Summary of Key Takeaways

As we come to the end of this journey through PowerShell, it's important to reflect on the key concepts and tools you've encountered. This book has aimed to provide a comprehensive understanding of how PowerShell can empower IT professionals to automate, optimize, and transform their daily tasks. Let's take a moment to recap the most important lessons you've learned:

1. **Understanding PowerShell Fundamentals:**
   - What PowerShell Is: You've learned that PowerShell is more than just a command-line tool. It is a robust scripting environment designed to handle complex IT automation and system management tasks.
   - PowerShell Syntax: The foundation of any good PowerShell script is an understanding of its

syntax, from cmdlets and pipelines to aliases and variables. Mastering the basics allows you to build more advanced scripts that can tackle real-world IT challenges.

2. Core PowerShell Concepts and Language Features:

- You explored how to work with *variables*, *data types*, and *control flow*, enabling you to write efficient and effective scripts.
- You learned how to handle objects—PowerShell's core data structure—and use cmdlets like `Get-Help`, `Get-Command`, and `Get-Member` to dig deeper into objects and their properties.
- The use of *functions* helped you modularize your code, making it more reusable and maintainable.

3. Automating IT Tasks with PowerShell:

- Automation is where PowerShell truly shines. From managing files and directories to working with the Windows registry, processes, and services, you've seen how PowerShell allows you to streamline routine IT operations, reducing the potential for human error.
- Task scheduling and automation have been demystified, showing you how to create powerful, time-saving automation solutions for regular IT maintenance tasks.

4. Troubleshooting Servers with PowerShell:
- You learned how to troubleshoot network issues, disk and storage problems, and monitor server health using PowerShell's built-in cmdlets. The tools to *query event logs, identify performance bottlenecks,* and *automate common troubleshooting tasks* are now at your fingertips, enabling you to maintain optimal system performance proactively.

5. Managing Users and Active Directory:
- Active Directory management is simplified with PowerShell. You now know how to create and manage users, automate Active Directory tasks, and query data from AD, allowing you to handle user accounts and groups at scale.
- You also explored Active Directory health checks and bulk user management, helping you administer large networks with ease.

6. Reporting and Auditing:
- You've learned how to automate the generation of system, security, and performance reports. PowerShell has given you the ability to export data to CSV, HTML, and PDF formats, ensuring that you can deliver actionable insights to key stakeholders.

- Additionally, you have discovered how to *track security logs*, *monitor user activity*, and *automate security audits*, which is vital for compliance in large IT environments.

7. Best Practices and Advanced Techniques:
- As you advanced, you explored best practices for writing clean, maintainable scripts, the importance of version control with Git, and *error handling* strategies.
- You also delved into *advanced topics* like PowerShell Remoting, cloud automation, building custom modules, and *integrating PowerShell with APIs and web services*, expanding your skill set to include some of the most powerful features of PowerShell.

8. Real-World Applications:
- Finally, we explored how PowerShell can be applied in real-world case studies. From *automating daily IT maintenance* to troubleshooting performance bottlenecks and managing thousands of Active Directory accounts, you've seen firsthand how PowerShell can be used to solve complex problems and save time across IT operations.

How to Continue Your PowerShell Journey

PowerShell is a powerful tool, but like any tool, it takes time and practice to master. Now that you've built a strong foundation, it's time to continue your PowerShell journey and deepen your expertise. Here are some resources that can help you take the next steps:

1. Official Documentation:
- The official Microsoft PowerShell documentation is the best place to start when looking for in-depth information on cmdlets, modules, and PowerShell features. The documentation is continually updated to reflect new versions of PowerShell. - Visit: https://docs.microsoft.com/en-us/powershell/

2. Community Forums:
- PowerShell has a vibrant, active community. The PowerShell subreddit and the PowerShell Discord server are excellent places to interact with other professionals, ask questions, and share your knowledge.
- PowerShell forums such as PowerShell.org offer valuable insights, tutorials, and troubleshooting advice from experienced users.

3. Blogs and Websites:

- There are countless blogs and personal websites that provide PowerShell tips, tricks, and tutorials. Some popular blogs include:
  - [Hey, Scripting Guy! Blog](https://devblogs.microsoft.com/scripting/)
  - [PowerShell Magazine](https://powershellmagazine.com/)
  - [PowerShell.org](https://powershell.org/)

4. **Books for Further Learning:**
   - If you're ready for more advanced PowerShell topics, consider picking up books that delve deeper into scripting, automation, and administration, such as:
   - "PowerShell in Depth" by Don Jones, Jeffrey Hicks, and Richard Siddaway.
   - "Learn Windows PowerShell in a Month of Lunches" by Don Jones and Jeffrey Hicks.

5. **Online Courses:**
   - Platforms like Pluralsight, Udemy, and LinkedIn Learning offer PowerShell courses ranging from beginner to advanced. These courses provide hands-on experience and can help solidify the concepts you've learned.

6. **GitHub Repositories:**
   - Explore open-source PowerShell scripts and modules on GitHub. By contributing to or

reviewing community-driven projects, you'll gain insight into real-world applications of PowerShell and expand your knowledge.

Encouragement to Experiment and Automate

Now that you've equipped yourself with a powerful set of tools, it's time to start experimenting. The best way to truly master PowerShell is by applying it to your own IT tasks and challenges. Start small with automating everyday tasks and gradually work your way up to more complex projects. Don't be afraid to make mistakes—each failure is an opportunity to learn and refine your skills.

Consider automating tasks you deal with frequently, like server health checks, file system management, or user account maintenance. With PowerShell, you can turn repetitive tasks into streamlined processes, saving you time and ensuring consistent, reliable results.

As you get more comfortable, explore *advanced automation scenarios* such as:
- Automating cloud infrastructure management (Azure, AWS, etc.)
- Creating custom PowerShell modules to extend functionality

- Integrating PowerShell with APIs to interact with web services and third-party applications

The possibilities are endless. PowerShell can become the backbone of your IT operations, transforming the way you work by enabling automation, reducing manual effort, and increasing operational efficiency.

PowerShell isn't just a tool—it's a game changer. Whether you're an IT professional, system administrator, or just someone interested in optimizing workflows, PowerShell offers a level of control and automation that can significantly improve your day-to-day tasks. As you continue to learn and experiment, you'll find that PowerShell becomes more than just a scripting language; it becomes an essential skill that empowers you to solve problems, streamline processes, and take control of your IT environment.

Remember that **practice makes perfect**, and **automation is the key** to efficiency in IT. Don't hesitate to apply what you've learned here to your daily work. Start small, experiment, and soon you'll be creating powerful scripts that save time, reduce errors, and boost your productivity. The more you practice, the more you'll discover the true potential of PowerShell.

We've covered a lot of ground in this book, but this is just the beginning of your PowerShell journey. Keep exploring, keep learning, and keep automating. The power to transform IT operations is in your hands—go ahead and make it happen.

Good luck, and happy scripting!

Appendix

A: PowerShell Cmdlet Reference

This appendix serves as a quick reference guide to some of the most commonly used PowerShell cmdlets that you will encounter in this book. These cmdlets are the building blocks of your PowerShell scripts and automations. Knowing how and when to use them is essential to becoming a proficient PowerShell user.

1. System Cmdlets
- `Get-Process`: Lists all the processes running on a system.

```powershell
Get-Process
```

- `Stop-Process`: Stops a running process by name or ID.

```powershell
Stop-Process -Name "notepad"
```

- `Get-Service`: Retrieves the status of all services or specific services.

```powershell
Get-Service
Get-Service -Name "wuauserv"
```

- `Start-Service`: Starts a stopped service.

```powershell
Start-Service -Name "wuauserv"
```

- `Set-Service`: Changes the properties of a service.

```powershell
Set-Service -Name "wuauserv" -StartupType Automatic
```

2. File and Directory Cmdlets

- `Get-ChildItem`: Retrieves items (files and folders) in the current directory or a specified path.

```powershell
Get-ChildItem C:\Users
```

- `Copy-Item`: Copies a file or directory.

```powershell
Copy-Item -Path "C:\temp\file.txt" -Destination "C:\backup"
```

- `Move-Item`: Moves a file or directory.

```powershell
Move-Item -Path "C:\temp\file.txt" -Destination "C:\archive"
```

- `Remove-Item`: Deletes a file or directory.

```powershell
Remove-Item -Path "C:\temp\file.txt"
```

3. User and Active Directory Cmdlets

- `Get-ADUser`: Retrieves information about a specific Active Directory user.

```powershell
Get-ADUser -Identity "jdoe"
```

- `New-ADUser`: Creates a new Active Directory user.

```powershell
New-ADUser -SamAccountName "jdoe" -UserPrincipalName "jdoe@domain.com"
```

- `Set-ADUser`: Modifies the properties of an existing user.

```powershell
Set-ADUser -Identity "jdoe" -Title "System Admin"
```

- `Add-ADGroupMember`: Adds users to an Active Directory group.

```powershell
Add-ADGroupMember -Identity "Admins" -Members "jdoe"
```

4. **Network Cmdlets**
   - `Test-Connection`: Sends ICMP echo requests to test connectivity to a host (similar to `ping`).

```powershell
Test-Connection -ComputerName "google.com"
```

- `Test-NetConnection`: A more advanced version of `Test-Connection`, with additional options.

```powershell
Test-NetConnection -ComputerName "google.com" -Port 80
```

5. Event Log Cmdlets

- `Get-EventLog`: Retrieves event log entries from the system's event log.

```powershell
Get-EventLog -LogName Application -Newest 10
```

- `Clear-EventLog`: Clears a specified event log.

```powershell
Clear-EventLog -LogName Application
```

6. **Scheduling Cmdlets**
   - `New-ScheduledTaskTrigger`: Creates a trigger for a scheduled task.
   ```powershell
   $trigger = New-ScheduledTaskTrigger -Daily -At "9:00AM"
   ```

   - `Register-ScheduledTask`: Registers a new scheduled task.
   ```powershell
   Register-ScheduledTask -Action $action -Trigger $trigger -TaskName "BackupTask"
   ```

B: PowerShell Error Handling

PowerShell provides several mechanisms for handling errors, ensuring that your scripts run smoothly even when unexpected conditions arise. Here are some key concepts:

1. **Error Types**
   - Terminating Errors: These stop the execution of the script immediately and trigger the error handling routine.
   - Non-Terminating Errors: These don't stop script execution and can be handled with `Try` / `Catch` blocks.

2. **Try / Catch / Finally**

```powershell
Try {
  # Try to run risky code
  $result = Get-Process -Name "NonExistentProcess"
} Catch {
  # Handle error
  Write-Host "Error: $_"
} Finally {
  # Always execute this block, whether an error occurred or not
  Write-Host "Execution complete."
}
```

3. **Error Variables**
   - `$Error`: Stores a list of recent errors.
   - `$?`: Returns `$true` if the last command succeeded, or `$false` if it failed.

- `$ErrorActionPreference`: Controls the behavior when a non-terminating error occurs. Set to `Stop`, `Continue`, or `SilentlyContinue`.

```powershell
$ErrorActionPreference = "Stop"
```

C: PowerShell Script Template

This is a basic template to help you get started with PowerShell scripting. Use this template as a foundation when creating your own scripts.

```powershell
# Script Name: MyScript.ps1
# Description: This script automates system maintenance tasks.
# Author: [Your Name]
# Date: [Date]

# Variables
$logFile = "C:\Logs\ScriptLog.txt"
$serverList = Get-Content -Path "C:\Servers.txt"

# Function: Write log
function Write-Log {
  param (
    [string]$message
  )
  $date = Get-Date -Format "yyyy-MM-dd HH:mm:ss"
  $logMessage = "$date - $message"
  Add-Content -Path $logFile -Value $logMessage
}
```

```
# Main Process
foreach ($server in $serverList) {
    Write-Log -message "Starting task on $server"
    # Example of running a task on remote server
        Invoke-Command -ComputerName $server -ScriptBlock {
        # Perform some task
        Get-Process
    }
    Write-Log -message "Completed task on $server"
}
...
```

D: Troubleshooting PowerShell Scripts

Here are some common troubleshooting steps when working with PowerShell scripts:

1. Check for Syntax Errors: Ensure that your script doesn't have any typos or missing brackets.

2. Use `Write-Host` or `Write-Output` for Debugging: These cmdlets are helpful for printing variable values and intermediate results in your script.

3. **Use `Set-PSDebug -Trace 1`:** This enables script tracing and shows the flow of execution.

4. **Check `$Error` for Details:** If a command fails, check the `$Error` variable for more information.

5. **Try `-Verbose` Flag:** Many cmdlets support the `-Verbose` flag to output additional details about the execution.

```powershell
Get-Service -Name "wuauserv" -Verbose
```

E: Useful PowerShell Resources

To continue your learning and enhance your PowerShell skills, here are some additional resources:

1. **PowerShell Documentation:** The official documentation from Microsoft is the most reliable source for cmdlet syntax and examples.
   - [PowerShell Documentation](https://docs.microsoft.com/en-us/powershell/)

2. **PowerShell YouTube Channels:** Several YouTube channels provide free tutorials and tips on PowerShell scripting.
   - PowerShell.org Channel: Offers regular PowerShell video tutorials and conference sessions.

3. **Books:**
   - "PowerShell in Depth" by Don Jones, Jeffrey Hicks, and Richard Siddaway is a great resource for mastering advanced PowerShell features.
   - "Learn Windows PowerShell in a Month of Lunches" by Don Jones and Jeffrey Hicks is excellent for beginners.

4. **Forums:**
   - [PowerShell Subreddit](https://www.reddit.com/r/PowerShell/): A great community for quick help and discussions.
   - [PowerShell.org](https://powershell.org/): A leading website for PowerShell tutorials and discussions.

This *Appendix* should serve as a handy reference for you as you continue to develop your PowerShell skills. It provides quick access to common cmdlets, error handling strategies, scripting templates, troubleshooting techniques, and additional resources to support your learning journey.

About the Author

Richard B. Statler is a highly experienced IT professional and systems automation expert with over two decades of hands-on experience in managing IT infrastructure, optimizing workflows, and streamlining operations. His deep knowledge spans a broad spectrum of IT technologies, with a particular focus on PowerShell scripting, automation, and system administration.

Over the years, Richard has worked in a variety of industries, from small businesses to multinational corporations, developing innovative solutions to simplify complex tasks and enhance operational efficiency. His passion for automation and problem-solving has led him to become a trusted consultant, trainer, and mentor for IT professionals seeking to improve their technical skills and embrace automation.

Richard has a talent for making complex technical concepts accessible to both beginners and advanced users. His writing style is practical and approachable, with a focus on real-world applications and actionable advice. He has authored numerous guides, articles, and training materials, contributing extensively to online forums, tech communities, and blogs.

Beyond his technical expertise, Richard is a strong advocate for continuous learning and professional development. He regularly engages with the IT community, encouraging others to embrace the power of automation to drive efficiency and innovation. In his spare time, he enjoys mentoring aspiring IT professionals and exploring new technologies.

Richard currently resides in New York, where he continues to explore new ways to harness the potential of PowerShell and automation to transform IT operations. When not immersed in technology, he enjoys reading and researching.

www.ingramcontent.com/pod-product-compliance
Lightning Source LLC
Chambersburg PA
CBHW071017240526
45469CB00006BD/1948